PROCESSING THE PAIN OF HEARTBREAK.

if you love someone . . . .

SEAN CURRY

FINDING THE REDEMPTION PLAN GOD HAS FOR YOU.

CONTENTS

~

THE REALIZATION

∽

It's over. It's really over. The next morning you wake up and realize that the nightmare—that you had hoped stayed in your bed—woke up with you. It's a very surreal feeling, isn't it? The mixture of confusion, of heartache, of fear, and of mourning. All to add up to the reality that your heart hurts. You are in pain.

The insecurities and fears begin to kick in.

> *What did I do wrong?*
> *Am I even worthy of love?*
> *Why won't anyone choose me?*
> *Why does it always end like this?*
> *I have to actually start over again at some point?*

And then the thought hits you...

> *What if I don't have to start over?*
> *What if I could get them back?*
> *Is this worth fighting for?*

We all love a good love story, right? We want our lives, our love story, to look like the love stories that we have seen in all of the movies growing up.

We want that Ariel and Prince Eric kind of love, that Cinderella and Prince Charming kind of love, even that Shrek and Fiona kind of love. We strive for that, dream of that, pray for that, and believe that one day we will find that in the perfect relationship.

Ariel fought by giving up her voice. Prince Charming fought by finding the girl that lost her shoe. Shrek fought by rescuing his princess from a tower. They all got that fairytale love. So if I fight hard enough, won't I have that kind of fairytale love, too?

The answer is maybe. It's possible. You may be in a situation that you need to fight for. There may still be hope there. There may still be life there to chase after. A romantic gesture or an intentional chat may do the trick. It may not be over for you.

But the hardest realization to face, the reason that I am writing this book, one of the biggest fears that we have to battle is this: for everyone else, the fighting is over. There's no revival coming. **It's over.** And now it is time to figure out where to go from here. It's time to figure out where to find hope, where to find joy, and how to see past the pain we feel and find expectancy for the future.

Let me be up front with you. This is not a relationship book. This is not a "how to get back together" book. This is a book for people who are experiencing the brutal reality that something they loved has ended.

I want to use this to invite you into the process with me. Healing is a tricky thing to figure out. Letting go of someone is even trickier. But, I have discovered is that there is hope.

If you love someone...you have to be able to set them free. Sounds crazy, right? Sounds cliché, doesn't it? It isn't as easy as it looks on paper, and sometimes it looks really messy. So how can this cliché saying become a prison-freeing reality?

It is available through one place alone: rediscovering belief that God is always good and that He is a God of faithfulness.

If this sounds like something you need, let's take a journey together. Consider this less a book of me preaching at you and more a moment that I ask to process with you. My hope is to show you how God has a plan of redemption for you, and it may not be as far off as you think.

JESUS UNDERSTANDS

JESUS WEPT

B efore we get into how to walk down the road of healing, you need to know that Jesus not only understands what you are feeling, He identifies with it. In this first section, I want to walk through a few moments in the life of Jesus so we can begin to learn to walk the way that He did. As followers of Jesus, we want to ask the question: *Who would Jesus be if He were me?*

So who would He be if He were heartbroken? Who would He be when He lost the love of His life? While Jesus never went through a relationship ending, He did endure the emotions surrounding it. You aren't alone. He understands. Let me show you what I mean.

Let's start with a man named Lazarus. The story of the death of Lazarus is such an interesting story, especially when it comes to the interactions and reactions that Jesus has. Lazarus of Bethany was one of Jesus's closest friends. In John 11, Jesus hears word that Lazarus was sick, and not like "has a cold" sick, like deathbed sick. He is sick to the point that the sisters of Lazarus send someone to make sure Jesus knows about it.

3 So the sisters sent to him, saying, "Lord, he whom you love is ill."

Have you ever found out someone that you love is really sick? I would venture to guess you gave them a call, changed plans, and did everything that you could do to go see them and be with them. So naturally, Jesus would have the same reaction, right? He's God! He will just go and heal Lazarus, won't He? I'm sure that this is exactly what everyone around Him thought would happen as well. But Jesus reacts in a completely different way than that. Check out His response:

4 But when Jesus heard it he said, "This illness does not lead to death. It is for the glory of God, so that the Son of God may be glorified through it."

Wait... Hold up. What did you just say Jesus? Your friend, who you love, is on his deathbed and your response is that the illness he has doesn't lead to death?? What in the world is that? I'll be real. If I was in the position of Lazarus's sisters, I would be pretty upset and in disbelief.

If I were Lazarus' sisters, I would be like: Do you not understand Jesus? Did I not explain it well enough? You're the same dude who I saw heal people, the same man who brought the miraculous to so many everyday situations!

At this point, in the book of John, Jesus has turned a bunch of water into a bunch of wine, broke cultural barriers with a Samaritan woman at a well, rescued an official's son from the grips of death, helped the crippled to walk, turned some bread and a few fish into a feast for thousands to eat, walked on top of water, and opened the eyes of a blind man! He has built the reputation of miracle worker and life giver. Why would He treat this situation any differently?

But Jesus seems to just shrug off the statement that the one that He loves is sick and is basically like "Ehhh...well it doesn't lead to death..." Where is your miraculous power Jesus?! Why are you shrugging this one off?

There have been many moments in the seasons after breakups that

I have felt like Jesus was just shrugging off my pleas for the miraculous. Have you been in the shoes of Lazarus's sisters before? Have you wondered why the God of the Universe was ignoring your pleas for His miraculous power? Have you felt like the only thing that Jesus has responded with was "Ehhh...well it doesn't lead to death..."?

In John 10, Jesus makes some really bold statements about His character and who He is. He calls Himself the Good Shepherd, the one who lays down His life for His sheep. He says that He and the Father are one. These are words and themes that are all about pursuing the one who needs Him and the fact that He is God, so He has the power to make things happen.

So why didn't He? Why didn't Jesus come through?

This is a question that many of us have asked at some point, isn't it? I know in my life, Jesus has rerouted prayers to different answers than I was expecting countless times. And it can be extremely frustrating. God's plan may always lead to good, but in the moments when we can't see the end result yet, it just seems bad. We will talk about this a lot later on.

So back to the story of Lazarus. There is a very important detail that it is easy to miss here, but one that is crucial in seeing the character and the heart of Jesus.

Lazarus's sisters were expecting for Jesus to jump at the opportunity to show off His miraculous powers and heal their brother, and He didn't. I'm sure that everyone around Jesus, in that moment, was so focused on what He could do, instead of what he was currently doing.

Don't miss this. Look at what Jesus does here.

5 Now Jesus loved Martha and her sister and Lazarus. 6 So, when he heard that Lazarus was ill, he stayed two days longer in the place where he was.

Jesus hears that "the one whom He love" is dying, doesn't answer the call to heal him right away, and now He stays in the place where He was for two more days. He wasn't planning to stay there, until He heard about the news of Lazarus.

Some could look at that as an uncaring God who didn't actually have a heart for His people. But could it be that Jesus actually had a very intentional plan in sitting still? Notice that Jesus didn't begin to simply walk a different direction. He stood still. Why is that?

One thing that I have noticed about Jesus is that He never does things by coincidence. He doesn't make mistakes. When we are trying to figure out something that Jesus has done, or is doing, we often ask things like:

Is He making a mistake?
Is His timing off?
Is He being cruel?
Does He not care?

The reality is that "no" is the answer to all of those questions. To make mistakes, have bad timing, be cruel, or to be careless is against His character. What we instead should ask is this:

What is Jesus trying to teach me in this season of sitting in my pain?
Here is what is hard for many of us to swallow: Sometimes God allows for us to sit in our pain. I don't believe that this is because He is cruel or unfair. It is because He is trying to let you hurt so that you have to rely on Him, so that you can learn what He wants to teach you.

The story of Lazarus does not end in pain, however. Jesus doesn't stay standing still. He begins to move. And as He does, His disciples begin to ask questions. Still in shock that Jesus didn't jump at the chance to flex His miraculous power, it seems like His disciples are in the stage

4

of denial that we talked about earlier, so Jesus begins to reveal the purpose behind why He let friends and family of Lazarus experience pain.

> *13 Now Jesus had spoken of his death, but they thought that*
> *he meant taking rest in sleep. 14 Then Jesus told them plainly,*
> *"Lazarus has died, 15 and for your sake I am glad that I was*
> *not there, so that you may believe. But let us go to him."*

Jesus says that for the sake of believers, He is glad that He wasn't there. Why? So that they could experience the resurrection power of Jesus in a completely new way. So Jesus makes His way to Bethany to see His friend, who, just to remind you, He knows is already dead.

When He gets there, He instantly stands face-to-face with the sisters who had already pleaded for their brother to be healed. And at this point, Lazarus has been dead for four days. I would guess that they weren't thrilled to see Him.

A little too late Jesus! Where were you four days ago?

I can only imagine the feelings of anger, abandonment, hurt, betrayal, mourning, and grief that Martha was feeling the moment that she looked into the face of Jesus. I mean look at her reaction!

> *21 Martha said to Jesus, "Lord, if you had been here, my*
> *brother would not have died.*

Pause. Before we finish seeing what she says to Jesus, this is where a lot of our faiths end. At anger. At hurt. At hopelessness. We allow for circumstances to overcome our ability to remember what God can do. We allow for our time tables to carry more weight than the time table that God can have for us, which is usually better by the way.

But Martha doesn't allow for her pain and anger at the Lord to blind her from remembering His power. Look at how she finishes this statement to Jesus:

*21 Martha said to Jesus, "Lord, if you had been here, my
brother would not have died. 22 **But** even now **I know** that
whatever you ask from God, God will give you.*

But... I know. I have emotions, but I know the truth about who you
are Jesus. I'm angry. But, I know that you are good. I don't understand.
But, I know that I can trust you. I want this person back, but I know
that your plans are better than mine. I feel like you messed up. But, I
know that your timing is never late.

What if... What if this could be a way that we approached Jesus?
With completely validated emotions, expressing our anger, frustrations,
and not understanding. But, always ending in knowing who God is and
what He wants for us. Because when we remember who God is, the ways
that we can see Him move are endless. And look how Jesus responds to
Martha in this moment.

23 Jesus said to her, "Your brother will rise again."

But even in this moment, Martha's humanity doesn't allow for her
to understand the gravity of what Jesus just said.

*24 Martha said to him, "I know that he will rise again in
the resurrection on the last day."*

And Jesus is like...no, no girl. Let me lay this out for you. I'm not
talking about the last day. I'm talking about right now.

*25 Jesus said to her, "**I am** the **resurrection** and the **life**.
Whoever believes in me, though he die, yet shall he live,
26 and everyone who lives and believes in me shall never
die. Do you believe this?" 27 She said to him, "Yes, Lord;
I believe that you are the Christ, the Son of God, who is
coming into the world."*

So Jesus begins to make His way to the tomb and it seems like He's about to heal this man. But not before He drops a bomb on us, not with His words. He does it with His actions.

35 *Jesus wept.*

Just when we think we have seen an end to the mourning and the grieving…Just when we think that Jesus is going to bring life to a situation that is dead…He stops and He weeps. Why is this?

Is it because the weight of His friends death has finally hit Him? Because He regrets not coming earlier? I don't think that's it.

See, what I think that Jesus is doing in this moment is leading by example. He is showing that before we fast forward to the life that Jesus has for us, it is important to sit in our pain and allow for ourselves to mourn.

We love to fast forward through the stage of mourning, don't we? It is painful to sit in. It brings about emotions that make us reflect and process through emotions that it would be easier for us to forget.

Fast forwarding through the mourning and the pain of losing someone is like trying to tiptoe through a field full of land mines. It may work for a second, but one bad day can lead to an explosion. I think Jesus wept so that we know that it is okay, actually encouraged, for us to weep at the thought of losing someone that we love. I think that He is trying to save us from an explosion later down the road.

The God of the Universe took time to stop and mourn through His loss. I promise you that you can find time in your crazy schedule to mourn your loss too.

Jesus wept. But again, He doesn't stop there. He doesn't stop at the mourning. See, you should mourn. But you also shouldn't stay there. You can't. God has too much for you. He has too much life that He wants for you to see. Jesus allows for His mourning to fuel His movement. We need to do the same thing. Allow for your mourning to fuel your movement.

His movement begins by standing up and walking to the tomb. Sometimes that's the first step we need to take. We just need to stand up and walk. We may not have any idea where God is leading us or where we want to walk to next, but it is such an important step to stand up and start to walk.

Jesus walks to the tomb, where the body of Lazarus has been laying for four days. I won't go into detail, but can you imagine the smell of that tomb after the body of Lazarus had been decaying for four straight days? This wasn't like he had just taken his last breath. It had been a minute y'all. There was a stone in front of the tomb to keep the smell in and close the burial sight.

> 39 Jesus said, "**Take away the stone**." Martha, the sister of the dead man, said to him, "Lord, by this time there will be an odor, for he has been dead four days." 40 Jesus said to her, "Did I not tell you that if you believed you would **see the glory of God?**"

Jesus doesn't care about the circumstances surrounding the miracle, because He knows the glory of God that is about to be revealed. This is so important for us to remember! When we lose someone, sometimes we get caught up in the circumstances that surround the situation, when instead, we need to fix our eyes on the power of the glory of God that comes through our faith in Him. Jesus doesn't get caught in, what we tend to view as, impossibilities. We seem to forget that all things are possible through faith in Jesus.

Too often, we look at "tombs" we have in our lives and see the circumstances around them to be too far gone for the tomb to be broken.

Maybe you have battled depression for so long that you feel like it is a tomb that you will never be able to escape from. I have news for you today: *Jesus wants to roll away the stone.*

Maybe you don't believe that you are worthy of love. You think that it is for everyone else but you. The tomb of future love is sealed closed, never to be opened. Guess what? *Jesus wants to roll away the stone.*

Maybe you are sealed in a tomb of bitterness. Forgiveness is too far off of a concept for you to grasp. So, instead of moving on, you are stuck dying in a tomb of bitterness and hurt. Guess what? *Jesus wants to roll away the stone.*

Maybe you have intentionally sealed yourself in the tomb of pride. You don't want for anyone to know that you are not okay. You don't want anyone to see your weak spots. So instead of processing and healing towards the future, you are stuck in a tomb of facade and fake masks. Can you imagine this? *Jesus wants to roll away the stone.*

Jesus approached the tomb and He did exactly what He promised that He would. He rolled away the stone. But He didn't stop there. Now that the stone had rolled away, it was time for the real work to begin.

> *41 So they took away the stone. And **Jesus lifted up his eyes** and said, "Father, I thank you that you have heard me. 42 I knew that you always hear me, but I said this on account of the people standing around, that they may believe that you sent me."*

Jesus lifted up His eyes to the Father. Did you notice that even Jesus, who is God incarnate, didn't try to get through His mourning on His own strength? Did you notice that even Jesus, Savior of the world, knew that the miraculous comes from first lifting up our eyes to the Father?

We cannot miss this. Too often, we try our best to heal and break through our tombs of pain by fighting by our own strength. We try to power through the pain with a "put the team on my back" mentality. But when it comes to seeing God's glorious power shine through, He actually reveals the most when we sit at His feet, look up at Him, and know that He hears us and is about to flex His muscles.

In this moment, Jesus, and everyone around Him, experienced the glorious power of the Father shine through.

> *43 When he had said these things, he cried out with a loud*
> *voice, "Lazarus, come out." 44 The man who had died came*
> *out, his hands and feet bound with linen strips, and his face*
> *wrapped with a cloth. Jesus said to them, "Unbind him, and*
> *let him go."*

Will the real tomb raider please stand up? Jesus calls a dead man to stand up and walk out of the grave. And I love what happens next. Jesus has the linen strips, that Lazarus was bound up with, removed. Do you see what happened? Not only did Jesus free Lazarus from the tomb, but He made it so that Lazarus could leave His bondage behind. He walked out of the tomb alive and free.

Maybe you have experienced what it is like to be freed from a tomb in your life and you have walked out of the tomb alive. But could it be that you have brought some of the bondage out of the tomb with you?

Maybe you are free from addiction, but you bring the bondage of shame out with you. Maybe you have walked out of the tomb of an abusive relationship, but you have brought out the bondage of fear and not seeing yourself worthy of redemption.

I just want to be clear about the heart of Jesus for a minute. His heart is not just to bring life back into a dead love life. His heart is to set you free from the past hurt that you've been bound down with and for you to walk out of your tomb more alive and free than before you walked in.

Lets back track for a second to the initial reaction that Jesus had when the sisters of Lazarus told Him that Lazarus was sick.

> *4 But when Jesus heard it he said, "This illness does not lead*
> *to death. It is for the glory of God, so that the Son of God*
> *may be glorified through it."*

What if this actually wasn't a cruel response? What if this was actually a statement that led to something bigger than anyone could have imagined? See what I think Jesus knew when He said this was this:

Sometimes things need to die so that Jesus can show you the power of resurrection.

Jesus wants for you to see the power of resurrection in your individual circumstances, your individual prayers, and in your individual hurt. And sometimes He will allow for you to sit in the death of the tomb for a season so that when He sets you free, you leave in a new freedom and life that you had before you went in.

I'll end this chapter with this question:

How do you think that Lazarus remembered those four days?

Do you think that He looked back and saw the tomb or do you think that He looked back and remembered the resurrection?

I know that the tomb of loneliness and of heartache feels like it is never ending, but here is what you can find hope in… **Resurrection is on the horizon**. And when you look back at this season, the tomb will not define it. How do I know? Because you will be walking in the new life of freedom that God has laid out for you. It's coming.

THE VALLEY OF LONELINESS

∽

When I was little, I hated going shopping with my mom. She is an interior designer and brings that profession into the way that she shops and dresses. Every detail of every outfit has to be perfect. Her closet? Don't even get me started.

When I go shopping, I am the kind of man who is in and out as quickly as possible. Weird fact about me: I will set off an imaginary timer when I am in Target to see how fast I can get what I need and get out. When it comes to shopping, I am all about efficiency. My mom, however? The opposite. It is a hobby and a joy to shop for hours at a time and try on every piece of clothing imaginable. So naturally, growing up, shopping with her was my living nightmare. A *"This will take thirty minutes"* shopping trip turned to an easy three hours.

The worst part? I was young, maybe nine or ten years old. That young, I couldn't drive, meaning I was held hostage to the unknown timetable of my mother. That's not a fun place to be in.

After a while, I would get extremely bored. So, I would create games for myself to play. A personal favorite for me was a unique version of hide and seek that I invented. Here's the catch: I'd hide, and didn't tell my mom that she needed to seek. It was surprise hide and seek. She'd turn around and surprise! Your son is gone and in hiding. She didn't like the game as much as me.

There was one game of surprise hide and seek that I remember specifically. It was in a Macy's back in 2006. We were probably on hour two of the shopping trip and it was time to shake it up. As my mom turned to talk to a sales associate, I ran into hiding in the middle of a circular clothes rack.

As I hid, I quickly grabbed every sales rack clothing item and slid the hangers in front of face until all I saw was darkness. And there I sat, silent, still, for what felt like hours. As the time passed by, the game became less fun. The darkness seemed to overtake me. My young self felt isolated and trapped, with no way out. The craziest part of it was that the way out was simple: just move the clothes and step out. But my mind saw isolation and it froze. In that moment, I firmly believed that there was no way out.

When we are lonely, it can become easy for our minds to see isolation and freeze. The longer we sit in loneliness, the easier that thought becomes to believe and the stronger the wall to get out of it feels.

Loneliness is crippling. Loneliness is debilitating. Loneliness brings out the inner fear and insecurities that we don't like to deal with or confront. When we are confronted with loneliness, we feel, well, alone. But so alone, that we can be in crowds of people and it still feels like we are stuck in dark room with no way out. Loneliness can haunt your room every night and morning, as you long for someone else be there. If we aren't careful, loneliness can become a living nightmare.

I wish I could say that I didn't have abundant experience in this department. But unfortunately, loneliness has been one of the main valleys that I have consistently found myself in.

Loneliness has been the target that the enemy has put on my back, and he is really good at hitting it. It has cost me many nights of sleep, plenty of insecurities to take footholds in my thoughts, and many days of feeling trapped, even though I would constantly be around people.

What I want for you to know today is that there is a remedy for loneliness, and we will get to that. But before we can, we have to confront the approach that we take to conquering loneliness. We have to learn how to break out of fear and do what it takes to find healing and freedom.

In my loneliest moments, the loneliness that I experienced doesn't even come close to comparing to the loneliness that a woman in the book of Mark experiences for twelve years of her life. TWELVE years, (and I thought my few months were bad).

Mark 5 describes the pain and suffering that this woman had to endure:

> 24 Jesus went with him, and all the people followed, crowd-ing around him. 25 A woman in the crowd had suffered for twelve years with constant bleeding.

Imagine for a second being in this woman's shoes. She is suffering from a discharge of blood for twelve straight years. And what the text doesn't say is the cultural significance of this. See, in Jewish culture, if you were bleeding, you were considered to be "unclean". This meant that no one wanted to ever be around you. In fact, it meant that you were viewed as a walking stigma that every person would do everything in their power to avoid.

If this woman would walk on one side of the street, everyone else would run to the other side. If she would reach out for help, people would avoid eye contact. If they saw her in tears or in pain, they would fake conversations to avoid interaction with her. No one would wave to her, no one would talk to her, no one would pray for her. No one cared about her. Twelve years of her life were marked by abandonment, isolation, and loneliness.

See, this woman was known externally for suffering from a disease of consistently bleeding. But internally, I guarantee you that the disease that she could think of was the disease of loneliness.

When we are trapped in the valley of loneliness, no matter what the external circumstances look like, it can be easy to only see the disease of loneliness within. Externally, people may just see you as the dude that just went through a breakup or the girl that was heartbroken. And they may avoid you because they don't know how to help you cope or how to help you heal. And externally, you put on a nice face and act like it's okay. But internally, you are suffering from the disease of loneliness. This exactly the place that this woman found herself in.

If you were her, wouldn't you do whatever it took to find healing? Wouldn't you try anything to find freedom and get out of the loneliness that marked you? She tried so many avenues, but nothing seemed to work:

> *26 She had suffered a great deal from many doctors, and*
> *over the years she had spent everything she had to pay them,*
> *but she had gotten no better. In fact, she had gotten worse.*

This woman, tired of constantly suffering, started going to every doctor that she could think of. She begged them to find a way to stop her bleeding. She paid dollar after dollar on specialists and medical remedies, and nothing would work. Nothing would heal.

To make matters worse, every time this woman would try to find healing, her bleeding got worse. Her loneliness got worse. Another doctor, another "*I don't know how to heal you*", another amount of money wasted, and it only got worse. How defeating did that have to be? Imagine every time you tried to get better, you just got worse.

When we are trapped in the valley of loneliness, it can become easy to develop negative muscle memories. We keep trying to run to fix after fix and just get worse. It makes us lose all hope and like the valley of loneliness will be our home forever.

This woman ran to doctors. We may not be running to literal doctors, but when we are lonely, we all have "doctors" in our lives that we run to, don't we?

When you are lonely, maybe you run to:
The doctor of alcohol
The doctor of pornography
The doctor of serial dating
The doctor of drugs
The doctor of comparison
The doctor of overworking
The doctor of shopping

We think that there are earthly doctors who are going to cure the disease of loneliness that we are walking through. But what so often happens is we run to these doctors to find healing and not only do they not cure us, but they make the issue worse. Here is why: just like the woman in Mark, we use every "dollar" we have to find healing and freedom, and when it doesn't work, we are left drained and it just gets worse. Our "dollars" are the amount of resources that we use, the time we spend, the thoughts that run wild, the nights without sleep, the days on end where are pain is not dealt with. We use all we have left and run to doctors that can't do anything to heal, and are left hopeless and drained.

I don't know about you, but there have been multiple points, in the valley of loneliness, where I have been drained down to nothing, felt hopeless, and was left on my knees begging God to bring me out of this valley. We often pray that God would pick us up and take us out of the valley, don't we? But what if He intentionally doesn't?

...and what if it was something done in His goodness?

We pray for God to take us **out** of the valley of loneliness but what if Jesus was trying to teach you how to walk **through** it?

This lonely woman, suffering from a bleeding disorder, had to of felt stuck. No way out. As she reached for doctor after doctor, attempt to be healed after attempt to be healed, cure after cure, and it only got worse. When all hope had to seem lost, all options seemed exhausted, and it felt like there was nothing else that she could reach for, she had a new idea, something new to reach for. And this time, she was met with the miraculous.

> 27 She had heard about Jesus, so she came up behind him through the crowd and touched his robe. 28 For she thought to herself, "If I can just touch his robe, I will be healed." 29 Immediately the bleeding stopped, and she could feel in her body that she had been healed of her terrible condition.

There are multiple significant things that happen in just these three verses. The first is that the woman wonders into the crowd of people in the first place. This is significant because it is crazy that she did it. Imagine intentionally wandering into a crowd of people who have ignored you, disrespected you, saw you as dirty and untouchable, and outcasted you for twelve years. You would have to want to stay as far away from them as possible, right?

Imagine the murmurs that must have began as this woman walked up to the crowd of people trying to see and hear from Jesus. Imagine the whispers of *"Why is she here? Ew, I hope she doesn't touch me. Who invited her? She doesn't belong. No one, not even Jesus, would want her to be near them.*" These comments and looks of disgust had to be something that this woman had become numb to, at the point.

She had this stigma around her that labeled her as unclean, remember? As she approached the crowd, I'm sure people began to get out of the way. And she kept walking, her eyes fixed on Jesus. People got out of the way because they were nervous to be tainted by the uncleanliness of the woman. But all the woman cared about was getting close to Jesus.

What happens next is what we so often miss, as we feel stuck in the valley. All options spent, all hope lost, the woman had one final idea on how to find healing. She ran up to Jesus and dove, through a crowd, to touch his robe. She believed that if she would touch His robe, she would find the healing that she couldn't find anywhere else. She saw the miraculous power that He had, had heard countless stories of the way that He had healed, and knew who He had claimed to be. So, she believed that He could actually heal her.

She dove. She touched his robe. And she was healed. The blood dried up. But the blood stopping was not the only thing that was healed in that moment. The stigmas that she had to face for twelve years were lifted. The disease of isolation and abandonment were cured. The valley of loneliness was climbed out of.

After going to doctor after doctor, spending dollar after dollar, and waiting year after year, she only getting worse. But Jesus brought complete healing. Friend, stop running to other doctors. Stop waiting for something else to work. What if you changed your approach from running after hopeful fixes and began running after Jesus? In our loneliness, we need to reach for the robe of Jesus. After all, He is the Great Physician.

Let me ask you: Have you ever been desperate enough to find healing that you would dive for the robe of Jesus? Have you longed for healing so much, to the point where you would confront your biggest fears, just to allow Jesus in? Have you developed a faith where you believed that if you would just get close enough to Jesus, you would be healed?

If you haven't, you need to know that the power of Jesus is available to you. There is no "doctor" with His power. Maybe it is time for you to dive for the robe of Jesus. He is the only cure for the disease of loneliness. And He welcomes your hurt, especially when it is met with faith.

> *30 Jesus realized at once that healing power had gone out from him, so he turned around in the crowd and asked, "Who touched my robe?" 31 His disciples said to him, "Look at this crowd pressing around you. How can you ask, 'Who touched me?' 32 But he kept on looking around to see who had done it. 33 Then the frightened woman, trembling at the realization of what had happened to her, came and fell to her knees in front of him and told him what she had done. 34 And he said to her, "Daughter, your faith has made you well. Go in peace. Your suffering is over."*

Daughter, your faith has made you well.

The woman touches the robe of Jesus and is healed. Jesus instantly feels "healing power" come out of Him. First of all, this would suggest that Jesus has more than one kind of power. He has healing power, but He also has resurrection power. He doesn't just heal, he brings what was dead in us back to life. He isn't just a temporary medicine kind of fix. He is a life changing, full healing solution. He doesn't just heal, he replaces your brokenness with life.

Jesus realizes that the power has come from Him. Now, don't forget, He is in a crowd of people. I'm talking shoulder to shoulder. I don't know if you have ever been in that kind of a crowd of people, but if you have, you know that when someone touches you, it is nearly impossible to guess who touched you. But not for Jesus. He asks who touched Him. His disciples think that He is losing it because they are like *"Dude, what? There are like fifteen people touching you at any given moment. You can't tell which person specifically touched your robe."*

The beautiful thing about Jesus is that He will never allow for you to be lost in a crowd. You may feel like there is never a time that you are seen. But if you reach for the robe of Jesus, He will always see you.

The woman calls out to Jesus and, **in fear**, says that it was her who touched his robe. She so desperately wanted to be saved and she knew that if she would just touch the robe of Jesus, she would find healing. But she was fearful. Maybe this was because she was so often reprimanded for getting close to other people. Maybe it was because she didn't fully know the character of Jesus or she was used to religious statutes instead of relationship. Maybe it was because she had been burned so many times before. I'm not sure.

But what I am sure of is that when we have faith, Jesus will never meet us with condemnation. He will meet your faith with a healing power of grace and love. You may be afraid, but **He will meet you with healing and comfort**.

All we have to do is stop running to other places and expecting to find a cure that only Jesus can bring. We need to stop burning out our resources on things that are just going to continue to drain us. In faith that He will heal, we need to dive for the robe of Jesus.

Tired of the valley of loneliness? Tired of feeling stuck, with no way out? Meet Jesus in your weakness and let Him give you strength. And when you do, guess what His response will be to you?

Go in peace. Your suffering is over.

Now you may be thinking: it can't be that easy. I have prayed before and my suffering is very much still here. I feel that. I have been there. Do you think this woman's life just magically was perfect? No way! She still had to mend and build relationships with her neighbors, rediscover her identity and worth, and learn how to live in healing.

The same will be true for you. The difference? Instead of being lost in the valley, you will have the light of Jesus to guide you through it to full healing. You may still feel weak. But the grace of Jesus will turn your weakness into strength as you fully heal.

There is a reminder of this, which I have turned to over and over again, as I have pursued full healing in Jesus. 2 Corinthians 12:9-10 explains that when you are healing in Jesus, weakness isn't something to be afraid of:

> 9 *"My grace is all you need. My power works best in weakness." So now I am glad to boast about my weaknesses, so that the power of Christ can work through me. 10 That's why I take pleasure in my weaknesses, and in the insults, hardships, persecutions, and troubles that I suffer for Christ. For when I am weak, then I am strong."*

The survival guide to your way through the valley of loneliness is the hope found in the Word of God. Run to it. Cling to it. Allow it to guide your weakness to the strength that Jesus is offering you. Be proud of your weakness, don't run from it. Why? Because, just like the woman did, when you come humbly before Jesus and believe in His power, you will be given strength.

Listen to the words of your Savior. Your suffering is over. The valley of loneliness isn't your home. It is just a place you are passing through. Allow for the healing to begin. The climb out of the valley is on the horizon.

THAT SINKING FEELING

∽

I love hiking. I get that from my mom. When I was younger, my family and I went to Zion National Park in Utah for one of my mom's big birthdays. We will call it her thirtieth so that she doesn't hurt me when she reads this. What you need to know about Zion National Park is that it s not an easy hike. Most parts are pretty strenuous. There are high cliffs, narrow walkways, high altitudes, slippery terrain.

As we were hiking one day, we came to a part of the trail where it was pretty difficult to navigate your next step. Picture this: on your left, there is a massive wall of rock. On your right, there is a canyon filled with rocks, only it is a four-hundred foot drop down to it. And the only pathway to prevent you falling is only around five feet wide. All that you can hold onto is a chain that is drilled into the wall of rock. Sounds fun, right?

Well, we crossed over this path. I didn't love it, but I made it. And we continued with our hike. A hour or so later, thunder began to rumble and the skies opened. We were hit with a storm. So we began to make our way back to the trailhead. Here was the issue though: we still had to go back over that slim trail of death. This time, however, it was wet, slick, and hard to see. We began to cross over it one by one, clinging to the small amount of support that we had in the chain attached to the wall of rock.

Because it was raining so hard, we couldn't look down at the rock to navigate. Instead, we had to keep our eyes on the horizon, what was in front of us.

When it comes to heartbreak, many times it is like being hit with a storm that you didn't see coming and feeling like you have to navigate an incredibly tricky terrain with very little support to hold onto. But, often, we get caught looking down at the place we are walking instead of the place that we are walking towards. And this is what makes us believe that we aren't getting anywhere in our healing, because we just see the scary terrain we have to navigate, instead of seeing the hope we are walking towards.

This reminds me of a moment that happens in Matthew 14:22-33, famously known as when Jesus walks on water. In this moment, the disciples of Jesus were in a boat, waiting for Jesus to catch back up with them. Directly before this occurrence in Scripture, Jesus takes five loaves of bread and 2 fish and feeds over five thousand people. Needless to say, I have to imagine that the disciples were in awe of what had just happened and it was fresh in their minds that Jesus was the God of the miraculous. You would think because of that, they would believe that Jesus could and would continue to do the miraculous. If they saw Him do something miraculous, they'd instantly have increased faith because of what they'd seen, right? Well...not quite.

> *22 Immediately he made the disciples get into the boat and go before him to the other side, while he dismissed the crowds. 23 And after he had dismissed the crowds, he went up on the mountain by himself to pray. When evening came, he was*

*there alone, 24 but the boat by this time was a long way
from the land, beaten by the waves, for the wind was against
them. 25 And in the fourth watch of the night he came to
them, walking on the sea.*

First of all, I don't want to skip past the fact that Jesus instantly
left performing one of the most miraculous events in history and then
spent hours in prayer, alone with God. Many of us don't like silence the
way that Jesus did. When we go through a hard break up and lose the
person that we love, it can be easy for our initial instinct to be to pack
out your calendars with busyness, to not allow for our minds to have to
sit in the hurt that we are experiencing.

But what if we could learn something from the times of solitude
that Jesus created for Himself? It would have been easy for Him to get
into the boat with His best friends and celebrate what just happened.
But instead, He knows the importance of getting alone with His Father
to refill. And that's exactly what we are searching for when we are in
pain, isn't it? To be *refilled*. We are used to our culture telling us that
the place to be refilled is by people or things of the world. So we pack
out our calendars, in desperation to find refilling.

What Jesus knew is that the only place to find true refiling was in
solitude with His Father. And friend, it may be time for you to take that
same approach. In that space, God may speak to you, He may refill your
joy, He may refill some peace, He may refill confidence in your identity
or calling, and at the least, He will hear you and refill your heart's need
for connection with Him.

Anyways, back to the story. Jesus spent so much time with His
Father, that it was now night. And the boat? Long gone. So did He
panic? Nah. Instead, Jesus made the water his sidewalk and walked on
top of it, out to the boat. Y'all. That is wild. But again, Jesus can do
the miraculous.

Now for a second, I want you to imagine what you'd think if you were on a boat, and out of nowhere, you saw a body appear out of the fog, walking on top of the water. Imagine what you'd say. Imagine how'd you respond. I wold imagine it would be something similar to the way that the disciples did:

> *26 But when the disciples saw him walking on the sea, they were terrified, and said, "It is a ghost!" and they cried out in fear. 27 But immediately Jesus spoke to them, saying, "Take heart; it is I. Do not be afraid."*

They freak out! They think that Jesus is a ghost, and clearly not a friendly one, like Casper. They scream out in fear. But Jesus looks at them, I imagine calmly, with a smirk on His face and says, "Hey, don't be afraid. It's just me."

> *28 And Peter answered him, "Lord, if it is you, command me to come to you on the water." 29 He said, "Come." So Peter got out of the boat and walked on the water and came to Jesus. 30 But when he saw the wind, he was afraid, and beginning to sink he cried out, "Lord, save me."*

Peter takes the bold step out of the boat to go meet Jesus in the midst of the waves. The boat was safe. The boat was comfortable. And most of the disciples chose to stay there, in fear. But Peter was different. He stepped out of comfort and into the unknown.

When we go through a breakup and lose the one that we love, it's like we have stepped out of the boat. Because whether the relationship was good for us or not usually doesn't define if it was comfortable. It was comfortable because it became what was known. There becomes a natural fear that develops to step out of that comfortable boat we've become used to and into the waves of the unknown. But, what if the unknown is where Jesus is standing. Notice Peter initiates stepping onto the waves, not Jesus. Jesus says to "come", but Peter had to put his eyes on Jesus first and tell him to command him on where to step. Peter takes the step, but Jesus guides the steps.

Don't miss what happened to Peter here. He was out of the boat, out of the known and the comfortable, but then the wind started to blow. With wind, comes bigger waves. And when bigger waves start to hit, your lives feel more unsteady and you lose your focus. This is what happens to Peter. The wind blows, the waves crash, and Peter loses focus. In this moment, he begins to sink.

I can imagine the thoughts that were going through his head.

I'm sinking. I thought I could trust you Jesus!

I should have stayed in the boat! Why did I get out?

This is not how I saw this going...

Help me! Rescue me! I'm drowning!

Lord! Save me!

When we step out of the known, the comfort of the relationship that we were in, I can promise you this: there is going to be wind blowing. There is going to be waves crashing. Your natural inclination is going to be to panic, and panicking causes us to lose focus on the hope that is in front of us. As much as I tell you not to, the reality is that you might. Why? Because the storm can feel unexpected. The wind can be stronger than we imagined it could be. The waves can shake our confidence and faith.

Lucky for us, Jesus knows that we may panic. Jesus knows that our eyes may fall off of Him. See, Jesus is God. He knows all. Don't you think Jesus knew that Peter would, even if it was just for a moment, take his eyes off of Him and focus on the storm? Don't you think Jesus knew He would have to save Peter from drowning?

And yet, Jesus still called Peter to step out of the boat. Jesus was ready to step in. He was ready to save Him.

31 Jesus immediately reached out his hand and took hold of him, saying to him, "O you of little faith, why did you doubt?" 32 And when they got into the boat, the wind ceased. 33 And those in the boat worshiped him, saying, "Truly you are the Son of God."

This is the good news. Jesus doesn't allow us to stay drowning in doubt, in confusion. He will always reach out a hand and take ahold of us. And there is something so beautiful in that, isn't there? That Jesus doesn't just extend a hand, but that He extends it and takes hold of us, even when our eyes have fallen off of Him.

Jesus grabs Peter. He saves Him. But He also addresses His doubt. He calls Him out for it. He says: "Dude, do you know how many times I have come through for you? Do you know the miracles that I am capable of? Stop doubting that there is something that I don't have power over."

Notice that when Peter got his eyes back on Jesus, the storm stopped. The wind ceased. The waves calmed. And Jesus led him back to stable ground.

Friend, I know that this heartache feels like a storm that you have no idea how to navigate through. There are days that feel like the wind is blowing three-hundred miles an hour and the waves have twenty foot swells. And the heartbreak goes from, what feels like a few raindrops one day to an overwhelming storm the next.

What I have learned in then midst of the swirling storms in my life is that the answer to calming the storm isn't by trying to swim harder. The answer isn't trying to get back to the boat, where I started. The answer isn't to hold my breath and hope that it goes away. The way that I have found peace and calmness in the midst of the most insane storms that I have had to walk through is by readjusting my eyes on Jesus and believing that He will do the rest. He will pull me up out of the water. He will get me back to stable ground. If you are stuck drowning right now, Jesus is reaching out His hand to grab you. Refocus your eyes on Him and allow Him to bring you back to a place of stability.

The last thing we need to look at is the response of the other disciples. After Jesus rescues Peter from drowning, He and Peter return to the boat. Think about what the disciples just witnessed! They saw their best friend drowning, in what looked like an impossible situation. And then they saw Jesus save him and bring him back to stability. (Not to mention, they saw Jesus walk on water.) What power!

Here's how awesome Jesus is: He not only has plans to rescue you from your storm, but He has plans to use your storm to show others the power that comes in fixing their eyes on Jesus. The other disciples worshipped and saw Jesus as the true Son of God. Did you know that walking through a storm creates a witness for you to others? Peter now had an experience that the other disciples didn't have, creating a testimony that none of them had.

Friend, there are people who see you right now. They see that the storm is consuming you. They see that you are drowning, just trying to maintain breath. And that can be the story that they remember. Or you could show them the power in refocusing on the person of Jesus and allowing Him to get you back to stable ground. From storm to stable ground, because of the power of Jesus. What if that story in your life would lead to someone else worshipping Jesus and seeing Him as the true Son of God? See, through Jesus our trials can be repurposed for life. We will hit more on that soon.

To close out this chapter, I just want you to encourage you to take a moment to mediate on the words of this Psalm of David. Know that these are the words that describe God's approach to you.

Psalm 18:16-19:

16 He reached down from heaven and rescued me;
he drew me out of deep waters.

17 He rescued me from my powerful enemies,
from those who hated me and were too strong for me.
18 They attacked me at a moment when I was in
distress, but the Lord supported me.
19 He led me to a place of safety; he rescued me
because he delights in me.

Jesus delights in you. He loves you. No storm scares Him. No winds are too strong, not waves too big. His hand is reached out to grab you. Just fix your eyes on Him, He will rescue you and bring you to stable ground.

BAND-AIDS DON'T FIX BULLET HOLES

∽

Have you ever had a dream car? Maybe you like to go fast and it's some kind of sports car. Maybe you're country and it's a pick-up truck. Maybe you're a flower child and it's a VW bug. Maybe you're environmentally conscious and it's a smart car. Maybe you're the opposite and it's a hummer. I don't know what it is for you. But for me, it was, and always will be, a Jeep Wrangler.

That is not the car I started out with though. My first car was a hand-me-down 1994 Jeep Grand Cherokee with almost 200,000 miles on it. It was on its last leg. In fact, about eight months into having this car, there was a morning that my mom asked me to go get her Starbucks. And when mom asks, you go. Now I had just woken up, so I was in Superman pajama pants, a t-shirt, and barefoot. And in my mind, I thought "well I don't need to get ready, I will just go through the drive thru real quick." So I hopped in the hand-me-down Jeep and headed out. But as I stopped to make a turn, I heard a loud noise and the car wouldn't move. The transmission had broken. The car was done. So here I am, Superman pajamas and no shoes, in the middle of a busy road, pushing my car to the side of the road. From there, my superman pajama pants flew all the way to a car repair shop and didn't return home for five more hours. Moral of the story? Wear shoes and put on real pants when you run to Starbucks.

With the car being dead and gone, my parents helped me out and blessed me. A couple weeks later, I had some friends over, and my dad came driving up the driveway with a 2016 black, soft top Jeep Wrangler. I don't think I can put into words my excitement. She was beautiful. I named her Baby, kind of weird... I know. But I drove Baby around everywhere. And you best believe that the top was down nine times out of ten.

One day, my friend and I decided to go see a movie. It was a beautiful Saturday afternoon. As we got to the theater, there was not a cloud in the sky. So, I left the top down. Surely this was a good judgement call. A couple of hours later, the movie had ended. And as we walked out of the theater, I heard the tragic sound of thunder. It was pouring; just my luck. My seats were soaked already, dash board dripping wet, puddles on the floor. So my friend and I made the executive decision to go ahead and just drive home, top down, in the pouring rain. Sometimes I have bad ideas... This was one of them.

As we drove home, it only started to rain harder. Lightning was everywhere. Simply put: we were not getting that top up. We were stuck in a rough place with no refuge in sight. But as we drove further, getting caught at light after light, we became desperate for refuge from the storm that we were in. It was a hopeless feeling.

When we face heartbreak, it can feel like we are caught in the rain, in need of refuge. Heartbreak can feel like one of the most helpless and hopeless feelings. Maybe that's where you are right now. Maybe you feel like you have a cloud that is continually floating above your head, pouring down rain, blocking out the sun, distracting you with loud sounds of thunder, and creating fear with each strike of lightning. You try to run but it feels like the dark place that you are in is impossible to escape. If you are like I was in that season, you feel worn down, tired, and burnt out. You feel like there is no escape. You are desperate for refuge.

The definition of refuge is this: "*shelter or protection from danger or distress*". When we are in danger, it is natural to seek after shelter. When our world is spinning, our heart longs for a refuge to calm the storm inside of us and the chaos around us.

The book of Psalms maps out how to approach the Heart of God in true vulnerability, in joy, and in mourning. Throughout the Psalms, the blueprint of the Heart of God is written. David wrote a Psalm that's so applicable to what we need to hear and believe as we find ourselves in storms. Psalm 18:30 reveals this beautiful promise:

> *This God—his way is perfect; the word of the Lord proves true; he is a shield for all those who take refuge in him.*

He is a shield for those who take refuge. A shield. The enemies goal for your life is to kill, to steal, and to destroy. Maybe you feel like there are things that are being stolen from you right now, killed off, or destroyed. God's promise to you is that He will be a shield of protection. But how do we access this shield? We must learn how to be a refugee. One who has been invited to seek shelter in the presence of the most high God.

When I was in the midst of the most brutal seasons of processing my heartbreak, I didn't know where to turn. I didn't know who to confide in. My trust levels were at an all-time low. I turned to friends, my family, some mentors of mine, and they were great support. But, I was longing for refuge, not just band-aids of fun, venting, laughs, and community.

As the great philosopher Taylor Swift so wisely says: *"Band-aids don't fix bullet holes."*

We have to be honest with ourselves: heartbreak isn't a paper cut. It doesn't just sting for a second and then go away as fast as it happened. Heartbreak is like a bullet hole. It requires extreme attention. If it isn't healed in a healthy way, it can cause infection to our heart, infection to the love that is coming, and infection to our mental, physical, and spiritual health.

Unfortunately, heartbreak isn't a quick fix. There isn't a band-aid strong enough. It requires a surgery of the heart. Right now, God has something to teach you that will reshape the way that your heart functions in the future. For the sake of this, let's look at God as our heart surgeon.

God is in the business of fixing hearts. He always has been. In fact, in the book of Ezekiel, He promises a new heart for those who turn to Him. We can hold onto the promise of Ezekiel 36:26.

And I will give you a new heart, and I will put a new spirit in you. I will take out your stony, stubborn heart and give you a tender, responsive heart.

If we can be honest with each other, after experiencing heartbreak, it can so easily feel like our heart becomes stubborn and hard as stone, can't it? However, it doesn't ever start that way, does it? It starts with the bullet hole forming in your heart. Then your heart feels incredibly vulnerable. You feel pain. You feel hurt. You feel betrayal. You feel loneliness. You feel isolation. You feel abandonment. But all you long to feel is nothing. Because feeling nothing is better than feeling the pain, right?

Enter in the stubborn heart of stone. It becomes hardened to the possibility of love again, hardened to the possibility that God has a plan, hardened to thought that everything will be fine, and hardened to the possibility that there could be purpose in the pain. And this is where many of us can live for a long time. If we aren't careful, our hearts can stay hardened for years, even well into a future relationship that the Lord may have for us.

This is why God doesn't just say, "Hey, let me bandage up that bullet hole of hurt and put you back out there to have it ripped off again." Instead He says, "Child, I know your heart is suffering. Let me take that one. Let me give you a new heart. Let me take that heart of stone and replace it with a heart that is tender and responsive."

When a person is getting prepped for open-heart surgery, a doctor will run multiple tests before hand to make sure everything is clear for surgery. One of the tests that a doctor may request is called *Cardiac Catheterization*. This test is done to check for blockages in the blood vessels of the heart. If blockages are present, then the surgery may not be successful.

Before God gives us the new heart that He promises us, I often wonder if there are some tests He needs to run first. I would imagine that He does something similar to the *Cardiac Catheterization*. He checks for blockages. When we go through heart break, it can be easy to have some things that block the flow of life into our hearts. Maybe you have a blockage of bitterness that you haven't dealt with yet. Maybe you have a blockage of doubt in the goodness of God. Maybe you have a blockage from hope thatGod wants to help set free. In heartbreak, it can become so easy to develop blockages that can hold us back from experiencing the full life our heart is designed for.

Another test that is commonly run before open-heart surgery is an *Echocardiogram*. This is a test the surgeon runs in order to test the strength of heart muscles. The surgeon wants to make sure that the heart muscles are strong enough to handle the change that they are about to experience. An *Echocardiogram* can be referred to as an ultrasound of the heart.

As we seek the Lord for a new heart, God will do an ultrasound of the heart. He will look at what we cannot see to bring us back to the life He has designed us for. The heart muscles pump blood so that your body gets fresh oxygen and get rid of carbon dioxide. Essentially, it pumps in life and pumps out death. How are your heart muscles right now? Are they pumping life into your heart? Or are the muscles malfunctioning and pumping in death?

The strength of a muscle determines how strong it is under tension. In realty, a heart doesn't physically rip to build back up stronger. But the muscles do! If you have ever gone to the gym and lifted weights, what happens? You are super sore the next day! Why is that? Because your muscles have literally ripped and are in the process of growing back stronger so that you can lift more weight.

Strength isn't a natural word that you may be using to describe the state of your heart. I'm not saying that it will be one that you use to describe your heart in the next week, or maybe even the next year. But what I am saying is that God creates a way for your weakened, battered heart to rediscover its intended purpose: to breed life into your body. To get that place of life, we need to take the time to rebuild strength.

Another test that can be run by a hospital, in prep from open-heart surgery, is an *Electrocardiogram*. An electrocardiogram is used to see if a patients heartbeat is irregular. In other words, is the rhythm of the heart where it is supposed to be? Is the heart beating like it was created to? If the beats are irregular, it can lead to a life-threatening stroke or cardiac arrest.

When we lose someone that we love, it can often feel like it causes our hearts to beat irregularly, can't it?

You ever been around that person that claps off beat? Maybe you were at church, a concert, or in the car and there's that person that just ruins the song because there is nothing in them that can actually maintain the right beat or stay on rhythm? Well when we go through heartbreak, it can feel like our hearts are like that off-beat clapping. And we want it to stop beating off-beat. We want it to get back in rhythm, but often we don't know how to redevelop this rhythm.

So, how do we clear blockages, rebuild strength, and redevelop rhythm? For me, there has been one antidote that has worked and it isn't some complex, jump-through-hoops kind of approach. It is simple in concept, and extremely necessary in practice. Are you ready? Are you ready to have your mind blown at this antidote that can heal your heart and prepare you for the rebuild that God has planned for you?

Here it is: *Prayer.*

Are you okay? Have you picked up your jaw from then floor yet? Have you caught your breath from me taking it away with that insane, undiscovered truth?

In all seriousness, you have probably prayed before, right? This isn't some foreign concept to you. Heck, you have most likely prayed in the midst of the season that you are walking through right now already. I did. I prayed a lot but I didn't feel like it was doing what it was supposed to. My prayer never felt like it was moving the needle in my life towards the healing and restoration that my soul so desperately was longing for. Is that you today? Do you feel that too?

Could it be that it is because you are using prayer as an elementary tool instead of a crucial life line to healing?

As I mentioned before, when I was in middle school and high school, I took Spanish classes. And just to shoot it straight with you, I was no bueno. I was the kid that would "go to the bathroom" during tests and google translate in the stall so I could try to pass. Most the time, I wouldn't. Don't judge me…you're just mad you didn't think of it.

But because I lived on Google translate, the worst part about Spanish class was the times I had to speak in front of the class. They were called PBA's. What does that stand for? I have no idea. I just know I hated them. When I would have to get up in front of the whole class, my Spanish would sound brutal. It'd be so broken, so spotty, and probably made no sense. Ninety-nine percent of the time, I didn't even know what I was saying.

Maybe that is how your prayer life feels right now, if you are honest. Your prayers feel broken. Your timing feels spotty. And you feel like what you are saying doesn't even make sense. That's how I used to be in prayer. Ninety-nine percent of the time, I don't even know if I knew what I was saying. God probably was waiting in Heaven with Google translate thinking: "Oh, Sean is praying again? Get the app loaded and ready!"

I took Spanish for six years and somehow it remained at an elementary level. Nothing was coming together. And it took me way too long to realize that the reason it wasn't progressing was because I had isolated my practice of the language to a classroom, for a hour once a day. I couldn't become at all fluent in the language because my practice was incredibly inconsistent.

Does this describe your prayer life? Inconsistent? Could it be that you are missing out on the healing that God has for your heart today because you are neglecting to invite the Healer in consistently?

Prayer can't be something we only use once or twice a day for a few minutes. We have to treat prayer like a language we long to master. Do you know the best way to master a language? By becoming fully immersed in it!

In the summer after my senior year of high school, I got the opportunity to go on mission to Guatemala for a month. I had been before, but I was with translators and English-speaking teams. This time, it was only a small group of us and there were no translators. I was fully immersed in a non-English speaking world. So... I began to learn how to actually speak a language that I had "practiced" for 7 years.

It didn't happen naturally. It was very awkward at moments. There was confusion a lot. But, by the end of the month, for the first time in 7 years, I actually felt like I could communicate in Spanish.

It's time to fully immerse yourself in the language of prayer. Because when we do, the Word of God shows that it can lead to a posture of joy. See, through prayer, your Healer not only wants to heal what is broken, but He wants to replace it with a consistent posture of joy. 1 Thessalonians 5:16-18 talks about how we go about getting there:

> 16 *Always be joyful. 17 Never stop praying. 18 Be thankful in all circumstances, for this is God's will for you who belong to Christ Jesus.*

Verse 17 says to never stop praying. *But Sean, how is that possible? How is that realistic? Do you not have a job or a life? How in the world am I supposed to never stop praying? Like maybe you can talk a lot or something Sean, but I am more introverted. I have less words to give. Never stop praying?? That seems outlandish!*

What if I told you that this isn't as wild of a thought that it may seem to be on paper? Let's run it down.

We talk to ourselves a lot, right? If you are anything like me, you have a consistent internal dialogue going on. We internally sing song lyrics. We recount lines from Netflix shows in our minds, hours after we watch them. When we sit in traffic, we say words we do not care to admit we say. We wake up in the mornings, look at social media and we talk to ourselves about what we are seeing. When we look in the mirror, we say that we wish we looked better, or today we are having bad hair days. We constantly talk to ourselves about conversations we are about to have with someone or we talk to ourselves about the way we could have said something better in conversations we just had.

Are you getting the picture yet? You probably talk to yourself a lot. So what does it mean to never stop praying? It means to bring your internal dialogue to God. A way that a pastor I know says it is this: *Talk to God about what you talk to yourself about.*

Talk to God about what you are talking to yourself about. Our minds are immersed in thoughts. And maybe I am just really weird, but those thoughts are consistently the thoughts that I am speaking over my life.

We have so many thoughts. And often times, we allow these thoughts to control our lives. But what if we changed our posture today? What if, instead, we immersed our thoughts in prayer?

One of the practical ways that I will do this is by going to Target. (I mean C'mon. Who doesn't love going to Target? And I just gave you an excuse!) When I get to Target, I will go to the notebook aisle and buy a small spiral notebook. Then I will write *PRAYERS* on the front of it in Sharpie. This book becomes my survival kit, my roadmap, my diary, my release, my place of pleading, my go-to for rejoicing, and my account of tangibly seeing God's faithfulness.

I take this journal and I write all of my thoughts down. I take it with me everywhere I go so that I can talk to God about what I talk to myself about. I write down little prayers, little life updates, big pleas, random rejoices, and prayers so big that only God could answer. This practically helps me to see that God is bigger than anything that I could possibly walk through and is always faithful to deliver in HIS perfect timing, not mine. So I can trust in Him at all times, in every season, during every circumstance.

Friend, grab a journal and begin praying to your Heart Surgeon. Plea with Him. Rejoice in Him. Seek after Him. He is waiting with open arms, a ready heart, and power to deliver.

Consistent prayer makes way for the rest of what 1 Thessalonians 5 calls for. When we never stop praying, it makes joy in all circumstances a real possibility. Why? Because life will always be rainbows and butterflies? No. But because when our thoughts are constantly immersed in prayer, God takes the weight of what we are praying and we can allow the Holy Spirit to let us walk in freedom.

In the same way, when we never stop praying, it helps us to be thankful in all circumstances, even when it doesn't make sense. In Jesus, thankfulness isn't set on results of things that happen to us, but is set on the immovable firm-foundation that is the hope of the Gospel.

Is your heart in need of surgery today? Our Jesus is waiting with a cure that is way better than a band-aid. His desire is to make you new. Maybe you are in the season of preparation, but would you join me in walking in faith that newness is around the corner?

Like I said at the beginning of this section, Jesus identifies with every emotion that you are feeling and every emotion that you will feel in the coming days, months and years. The road to healing begins with understanding that there is a good God who loves you where you are at. He sees you. He hears you. He identifies with your weaknesses and He wants to walk with you to the future ahead of you. Notice I said it is a road to healing. It's not just a little jump, a snap of the fingers, or an overnight transformation. Healing is a journey, and it's a journey centered on Jesus. So, now that we have established that, let's start navigating.

THE ROAD TO HEALING

PAIN SUCKS

∽

kay, healing. Often times, healing can feel like such a lofty prin-
ciple. It can feel far out of reach. So, where do we even start?
If you just lost someone you loved, you are in pain. Let's start there.
Usually the first chapter of a section has some catchy title, with the
attempt to reel the reader in and convince them that this is going to be
worth their time. I thought about doing that, but here's what I believe:

Pain sucks.

Can we just agree on that? Cool. Glad we are on the same page. It
doesn't deserve a catchy title. It doesn't deserve to look good on the eyes
or sound good rolling off of the tongue. Pain simply hurts and it sucks,
so we are going to leave it at that.

I have played hockey for 17 years, and I used to take pride in the
fact that I had never had a serious injury. Never broke a bone, got a
concussion, or even had a cavity. When somebody would ask me a fun
fact about myself, I would always go with that.

I must have said it too many times, because shortly after, I ran into
a wall. A brick wall.

I was just an innocent seventh grade boy who loved to play frisbee. My teacher let us go outside one day, in the middle of social studies (can I get an amen?).

My friend and I began to throw and slowly, step by step, we began to get further and further away from each other. At this point, we were launching the frisbee, pretty much we were pros at that point, with dreams of the ultimate frisbee olympics. That's a thing, right? When I get competitive, I get real competitive, so I was not about to drop the frisbee. I was going to catch it, whatever it took.

And then the moment happened. The frisbee launched, I ran, eyes locked on the translucent red disc. I had the rough, worn plastic at my fingertips, just out of reach…and then I woke up in the hospital. I had run straight into a brick wall. Out for 45 minutes, gash on my head, major concussion. Most embarrassing moment of my life.

When you get a concussion, you go to the doctor, you get sleep, take some Advil and then you begin the process of healing. But, here's the thing: you have an end date for that healing. There's an expiration from that pain. Two weeks. Two weeks and your life is back to normal. The pain is over and you can go back to playing frisbee and trying to avoid walls.

As much as that hurt, it has nothing on the pain of heartbreak. Heartbreak feels like something constricting in your chest, like a gray cloud is following you, like your eyes are constantly burning from fighting back tears. Heart pain is a different animal, it isn't like any physical pain. It doesn't have a set expiration date.

And before we go any further, *if you are in pain right now, I am sorry.* You are not alone and your heart matters. No matter what anyone says, your pain is real and it is valid. Do not let anyone or any thought tell you differently.

If you have been there, you know of the confusion that happens when it feels like your heart has healed, you have found your redemption story, and one day—in the blink of an eye—you feel like you are back to square one.

In August of 2018, I was looking at wedding venues, had her father's blessing, had a ring picked out, and was so excited for the rest of my life. And, in an instant, all of that was gone. My heart was broken.

Here's a quick reminder, in case you forgot, pain sucks. In fact, the literal definition of pain, according to Merriam-Webster, is "an unpleasant sensation that can range from mild, localized discomfort to agony." The word *pain* is derived from the Latin word *poena*, which means a fine or a penalty. So often, pain feels like exactly that, doesn't it? A penalty.

When I got the call from who I thought would be my future fiancé, and she broke things off, I remember that exact feeling. Pain. The questions echoed through my heart: *Is this some kind of penalty? What did I do wrong?* And most importantly, *Why would God let this happen?* It feels like a punishment.

Have you ever been put in time out or been grounded growing up? When I was ten years old, my parents and I moved into a new house, which was under construction still. If you have ever been to a construction site, you know that there's a lot of very expensive and powerful tools present, such as a bulldozer.

Like many ten year old boys, I loved to throw rocks. I have always been a massive baseball fan and loved to pretend that I was pitching to win the Yankees the World Series. It would be the bottom of the 9th, no outs, bases loaded, the Yankees up by one, and I was called in to strike out the next three batters to win the game.

So, there I was, on top of a hill, called into the game. The strike zone in my fantasy baseball games was usually a tree, but, for some reason, on this day, I chose the window of the bulldozer. And on this day, I happened to be incredibly accurate.

The window was destroyed, glass everywhere. I went inside and hid in my room, knowing that the confrontation would come soon enough.

About thirty minutes later, a ring came at the doorbell. It was the contractor. And could you guess? He was not as thrilled at my World Series victory as I was... Must have been a Red Sox fan..

My parents called me downstairs and began to yell at me. What was my only response? But dad...I won the Yankees the title, aren't you proud? And through his semi-proud, yet unamused smile, he said that I was grounded.

I have to say I deserved that one. But when it comes to walking through the pain of heartache, it can feel like God is putting you in timeout, like He grounded you. But often times, it is tough to understand the reason behind it.

Often times, when you were grounded growing up, you had your favorite things taken away from you. Your phone, computer, video game system, time with friends, and for the Christian kids, even youth group, was taken away. And when you are broken up with, or lose someone that you love, it can feel like all of your favorite things are being stripped away from you, and you are stuck in isolation.

Back to that dreaded August... I felt like I had just been grounded, on steroids. All of my favorite things were stripped away: my best friend, my future wife, the future mother of my children, my excitement for my future, my dreams of marriage, the friendships I had created, the family I had grown so close to, what felt to be my everything—stripped away out of nowhere. My favorite things gone, leaving me in isolation and in pain.

They say that there is process when it comes to pain. And here is the thing with processing: it takes time. Processing takes dealing with the pain, sitting in it. Sitting in something that hurts is not a fun place to be in. Just like pain...it doesn't have an immediate release. But, it is something we must walk through to find freedom.

There is a cycle of grieving. Have you heard of this before? The eight stages of grief, or in other words, the processing that you have to go through to get to the point of moving on. Grief is a complicated and messy. It doesn't look the same for everyone. Not all people experience every stage of grieving for every situation that they go through.

The stages of grief were actually intended for the terminally ill, to process the reality that death was looming. As humans, we aren't wired to be able to process death or loss. But the stages of grief help us navigate what it can look like. These are not a box to lock yourself in, but a roadmap to process along the way to healing.

Obviously, in this book we are not speaking about physical death. But when we lose someone that we love, we have to learn to grieve the death of emotional attachments and plans that we had created. So grief stages can help us find a way to put into words the steps we need to take to move forward.

Throughout this book, we will process through these eight stages, because the reality is that you either are in one of the stages right now or will have to go through the full cycle in the future.

Grief Stage 1: **Shock or Disbelief**

Remember the first sentence of the book? Go ahead and flip back to page 1. The first feeling that you get when you lose someone that you love is the shock that the nightmare is real. You want to keep going to sleep so that you can wake up and see that the girl or the guy is still in your life and you just lived in some parallel universe for a few hours. But the nightmare is real, it's over. And you are left in shock.

And it feels weird because you may not necessarily be experiencing the pain that comes with loss yet. Your heart hurts, but you may wonder why you don't feel that hurt to the degree you know you should be. It's probably because you are in a state of numbness. A state of disbelief. Your heart feels numb. Your mind feels numb. Your emotions feel at a stand still. And one of the hardest things to battle, if we can be honest, is not allowing our faith to become numb too.

Numb faith is a faith that leads to other detrimental emotions. It can lead to feeling stagnant, stuck, or even death of faith. Maybe you have been or are in a season where your faith feels numb, and you are just looking at it as a "break". But here's the thing: "Breaks" from God can turn to broken paths for the future.

In Grief Stage 1, you are in a place of shock and disbelief. In the Bible, David was a man that knew a thing or two about seasons of shock and disbelief. Yet, he constantly intertwined them in faith. If you have ever read the Psalms, you know of the emotional rollercoaster that David goes on in his prayers with God. As we dive into the different stages of grief, I believe that his interactions and genuine emotion with God will be key to seeing what our response should be to God, as we go through each stage.

Psalm 13 is a great place to start as we talk about the questions that can come with shock. Because the last thing we want to happen is our hearts becoming numb. Look at these questions and the tone that David uses here:

> *1 O Lord, how long will you forget me? Forever?*
> *How long will you look the other way?*
> *2 How long must I struggle with anguish in my soul,*
> *with sorrow in my heart every day?*
> *How long will my enemy have the upper hand?*

Don't these questions sound familiar? I know that for me, these are questions that have echoed through my mind and heart consistently. But here is the thing that David does with these questions that I struggled for far too long with: *He asks them out loud.*

The thing with numbness is that it makes it easy to internalize questions and emotions. Everything on the outside is stuck in place, stone-faced, but the inside is running crazy, trying to figure out where to turn next, looking for answers to the questions that our hearts are fervently searching for.

This is an option. You can process this way and pretend externally, both with people who love you and with God, that everything is okay. It is an option. But is it the best option? Probably not. See, the problem with this approach is that it leads to stress, anxiety, bitterness, and ultimately a complete shut down from the inside, out.

David externalizes his pain. He lets God in on his confusion. He lets God in on His numbness. These questions are not questions that are masked with an *"But at the end of the day, I am okay"* kind of mask. He asks the Lord if He has forgotten David forever! This is not some light question to ask! It's heavy to believe that the all-knowing God that created you may have gotten to a place where He has forgotten you.

Doesn't David know that God is always good? Doesn't David know that the Lord is always with him? Doesn't he know that God will never leave nor forsake him? Is this David's faith being weak?

As Christians, when we face internal numbness and shock, and questions begin to build, we can face the fear and the lie that questioning God means that our faith has weakened, so we push it down.

Here's what I want to argue in this moment with you: Questioning God doesn't show *weakness* in faith, it shows **maturity**.

These moments of questioning do not mean that you're backtracking on your deep understanding of the goodness of God or His presence or His faithfulness. These questions are inviting the God of goodness into your numbness so that He can remind you once again of the feelings of peace, love, faithfulness, and even the feelings of hurt or of anger.

Externalizing numbness to God helps you to feel. You may not want to feel or show emotion. I know that men can feel that way often. But the truth is that God created each of us with emotions and they are meant to be used. Jesus didn't just smile and laugh. He also cried, yelled out in agony, and flipped tables in anger. We need to encounter emotion.

What is the emotion that you will feel? That is whatever God knows that you need to feel in order to heal. He knows what you are feeling, even when you don't say anything. But you opening up to Him, especially in your numbness, gives your heart a chance to feel what God has for you, instead of what the lies that come with numbness have for you.

Numbness is a lie that we can avoid the pain of the emotions that come with being in pain. It can be very tempting to stay numb. The lies of numbness speak that you can just breeze through pain and come out on the other side all good, no battle wounds. But the truth is that if you allow numbness to prevent you from emotion, you will have a much longer and unhealthy road of processing to walk down.

Shock leads to numbness. But real, unfiltered, vulnerable prayer can lead to a place of feeling that can break the stagnancy of grief stage one and move you closer to the freedom that God has for you on the other side.

Grief Stage 2: **Denial**

October 19, 2019: A day that I will remember for a very long time for many reasons.

First of all, it was the last night of my best friend's bachelor party, the night before his wedding. I was his best man, and so I was doing everything that I could to make it the greatest night that he could have as his last night being a non-married man.

Now, before you get thinking anything too wild, we are Christians so we ain't going Vegas crazy or anything. Our night was spent full of mini ice cream cones, a few beers, games, embarrassing stories of my best friend, and playoff baseball.

Like I mentioned earlier, I live, breathe, and bleed Yankees baseball. If you are mad about that, haters gonna hate. My 27 championships speak for themselves. Anyways, the Yankees were playing the Houston Astros in Game 6 of the 2019 ALCS that night. If you don't know anything about baseball, let me help you out. We do not like the Astros.

If you do, you won't speak up anymore because of all of the cheating scandals. Rant over. Can you tell there is still hurt there from that night?

It was the top of the 9th, one on base, one out, Yankees down 4-2, DJ LeMahieu at the plate, three balls, two strikes. The next pitch, he hits a game-tying home run to right field. I have never screamed in the pitch that I did in that moment…it was the equivalent to a dog whistle. The Yankees weren't done yet.

On to the bottom of the 9th, one on, 2 out for José Altuve (just saying his name makes me need a therapy session). On the fourth pitch of the at-bat, he hit a walk-off, game winning 2-run home run to left field. Series over. Yankees eliminated. Heart broken. Maybe that should be my next book: *Diaries of a Heartbroken Sports Fan*. I am a Knicks fan, after all. I have a lot of experience in that department.

The home run played on repeat in my mind the rest of the night, as I tried my best to stay somewhat joyful for my best friend. Did Altuve cheat? That's up for debate. Not the point. The point is that in that moment, I went through the stage of shock and disbelief pretty quickly and went straight into denial. To be honest, I still may be living in denial from that one.

When it comes to losing someone or something that you love, denial is a tough place to sit in. Denial can come in many forms. Here are a few **key lines** that may come up when you are faced with denial:

"I'm okay."

Let's stop here for a second and have a quick chat about this phrase. I know that saying "I'm okay" can come from a very genuine place of trying to move on. However, if you cannot come to the realization that there may be some parts of you that aren't okay, you are most likely in denial.

Next line: *"He or she will realize that this is a mistake soon enough and ask me to come back in their life"*

Let me be real with you. I have had this thought many times in this stage of grieving. It may be true that it's in God's plans for the person that you lost to resurface in your life. It may happen in a month, a year, or 5 years from now. But, it also may never happen. Unfortunately, we can never know. While I am not going to sit here and tell you that this thought will never be real, I want to tell you something that God has taught me. We are processing together, remember?

Here is what I have had to learn through a lot of pain, processing, and prayer: We can't know what the future holds, but we can trust God enough to let go.

They may come back, they may not. But, until we let go of expectations on either side of the coin, we will never be able to fully heal and fully surrender to Jesus.

Next line: *"This isn't happening to me."*

At face value, this feels like a silly statement. This isn't happening to me? Um, yes it is. That's why you are in this place of grieving in the first place. But when you are in grief stage two, this is not a silly statement that words can justify. It feels real. The disbelief that this is your life is very real. For the person that is grieving, it almost feels like they are living life as a character in a Netflix show. This can't actually be their life.

The thing with denial is that, at its core, it is a defense mechanism to cover the pain that we don't want to actually feel. It is common to block out all of the thoughts of reason because with reason, comes the realization of the heartache that we are trying to avoid.

So how do we combat denial? Find someone who you trust who can be honest with you about where you are actually at. My friend, Thomas, is that person for me. When I am in denial, Thomas will say things like: "Sean, she's gone right now bro. God has such a plan of redemption for you, but it is His plan, not yours. So let yourself realize that this is over, and invite Jesus in."

These are some of the moments that have helped me the most. They are not fun to hear. They make you want to get defensive and justify that things may not actually be over. But at the end of the day, I trust Thomas enough to listen to him, even when I don't want to. Find a person like that for you, and ask them to be real with you.

And here is the hard part: Listen. Sit with that person and say this line out loud: This is over. They are gone. This is over. They are gone. This is over. They are gone. It won't take away all denial in that moment, but it will help you to have a person and a place to process and begin to heal with.

Grief is not foreign to Jesus. Jesus didn't allow Himself to be above feeling pain. Actually, He makes a point for us to know that grief is okay to sit in, that it is a process of healing, that pain can not be looked past or ignored. We will talk about that in the next chapter.

Pain sucks. It is brutal. Nothing I can say will make that any less true or real. It hurts a lot right now, but it isn't your story. Pain is not who are. It isn't where it ends. I know that we are only in the first chapter. I know that we are only scratching the surface of where we will be by the end of this book. But I don't want to wait to tell you that pain is not going to define the season that you are in right now, the coming redemption will. Yes, it hurts. Yes, it is awful. But it isn't where this story will end.

With that being said, there is some more about pain that we need to understand, starting with the fact that Jesus understands and is in it with you. Hard to believe, I know. But let me show you.

SO, YOU'RE ANGRY?

ﾟ∾ﾟ

One of my all time favorite movies is *The Patriot* starring Mel Gibson and Heath Ledger. If you've never seen it, it is definitely worth the three hours that it takes to get through it. If you are like me and you love movies that mix a deep, emotional storyline with people's heads being blown off by bombs, there is just not a better movie ever made.

Now that I am expecting you all to go watch it, I'll try not to give away too many spoilers. The movie stars Mel Gibson, as Benjamin Martin: a used-to-be war hero turned a rocking-chair making man of the simple life. Life is simple farm life until the American Revolutionary War rolls into town. Benjamin doesn't want much to do with this, but his son Gabriel, played by Heath Ledger, has something stirring in him to fight. So Gabriel runs into battle with the British.

Through a series of events, Benjamin Martin sees that it is time to go fight alongside of his son, so that he can protect and get revenge for his family. They start by dominating battle after battle, seeming to be unstoppable. Until one battle against the "horse-riding red coats".

Spoiler time: One of the greatest fight scenes in the movie ends in absolute heartbreak as Gabriel is shockingly killed by the main "bad guy red coat", right after everyone thought he had been killed. Benjamin gets to the scene right as the British officer fled the scene, just in time to hold his dying son in his arms to witness his last breath.

I can only imagine the pain of losing a child. The heartache, bargaining, and grief must be on a whole new level. In no way am I trying to compare a breakup or separation to the pain of losing a child, as I know that pain probably does not even come close. But I do believe this: Any kind of traumatic heart pain begs the need for processing one's grief. Some pain can be more intense than other pain, but all pain is valid and needs to be processed in a healthy way.

We have already talked about the stages of shock and denial, back in chapter one. And the director of *The Patriot* seems to skip right past these stages too, as Benjamin watches his son, Gabriel, die. Benjamin heads straight into grief stage three.

Grief Stage 3: **Anger**

For the rest of the movie, Benjamin is straight-up pissed. The battle scenes take a whole new level as he seeks out the British officer who killed his son. He wants revenge. He wants blood. He wants for people to die.

And, interesting enough, we see this exact thought process occur in the Bible. In the Psalms, David ain't afraid to say what is on his mind, even if it means asking for God to kill some dude that he doesn't like! What??

Check this out, I'm not making it up. Psalm 109:6-13, look what David is asking to happen to this dude that did him wrong:

6 Get an evil person to turn against him. Send an accuser to bring him to trial. 7 When his case comes up for judgment let him be pronounced guilty. Count his prayers as sins. 8 Let his years be few; let someone else take his position. 9 May his children become fatherless, and his wife a widow. 10 May his children wander as beggars and be driven from their ruined homes. 11 May creditors seize his entire estate, and strangers take all he has earned. 12 Let no one be kind to him; let no one pity his fatherless children. 13 May all his offspring die. May his family name be blotted out in the next generation.

Can we just agree that David was angry? He is making some pretty bold and aggressive statements here. Not only does he want for his enemy to die, but he wants his children to be homeless, everyone to be mean to them, and all future generations of his family to die.

I bet you won't here this piece of Scripture in a sermon at your church anytime soon. But I think that there are some really important lessons to learn here.

So you're angry? *It's okay to be.*

When we lose someone that we love, there will always come a time, at some point, where you will make the switch from denial to anger. If you're anything like me, it takes a hot minute to get there. Like I said earlier, I am a fighter. I want to make things work, so the denial and the shock take a little time for me to get through. So for me, anger comes a couple months after the moment that the relationship ended.

There are different ways to process anger, some ways healthy and some not as much. A few months after the breakup that I went through in 2018, I decided to take up boxing. Punching heavy things for an hour and a half? Sign me up.

Going to the gym, boxing, and playing hockey were my biggest ways with coping with my anger. Did these provide great temporary relief from my anger? Yes. It gave a me the temporary release. Did they get me in better shape? Yes. But did they get me through the stage of anger? Unfortunately, no. They didn't. They were cover ups and temporary fixes to an issue that needed a lot more attention.

We are really good at being quick to find cover ups for our anger. And I want to be really candid for a second because I think it would be easy for me to skip over this uncomfortable territory and easy for you to not have to read or think about this. But how can we heal together if we don't process the uncomfortable parts of healing?

Before we dive into the remedy for anger, I want to spend a minute talking about the unhealthy cover ups that we can sometimes dive into.

The first unhealthy cover up? *Pornography.* That word can instantly bring tension into a room, can't it? It can male your hands sweat, for sure. But the unfortunate reality is that after we lose someone we love, this can be one of the most unhealthy cover ups that we can turn to. When we are in a tough place mentally, and anger begins to mix with loneliness, our minds can look for quick fixes of relief. Enter in pornography.

I believe that pornography is one of the main tools that the enemy wants to use to ruin the healing God wants to do in you. It will make you believe that you are not enough with only having Jesus. It will destroy the influence that God is preparing for you to step into.

Do not allow for the enemy to help you to justify pornography by falling for the lie that it will "just be a season". Part of healing is allowing God to shape you into the husband or the wife that He wants for you to be. Falling into a cyclical pornography addiction is the opposite of preparing yourself for a healthy marriage.

So get accountability. Get vulnerable with other men or women about the battle and temptations that you re facing. Find the healthy solution to anger, not the temporary detriment that is pornography.

Another "cover-up" that some people will use to mask anger is alcohol or other substances. Some people will disagree with me on this statement, and that's okay, but alcohol, when you are of age, on its own, is not a bad thing. But when it is used as a quick release, or a cover-up, for anger, it is incredibly dangerous. It can be a slippery slope to walk on. If you could see it becoming an issue, maybe you should go without it for the season of healing. Regardless, use that accountability partner to keep you accountable in the way and amount that you are drinking.

The Bible is very clear to be sober-minded. 1 Peter 5:8 says "Be sober-minded; be watchful. Your adversary the devil prowls around like a roaring lion, seeking someone to devour." When you are healing, you are in an incredibly vulnerable place. There is a real enemy waiting for your guard to be down so he can attack and hurt you. He longs to ruin all progress of healing that you have mind, The quick release of alcohol is not worth the susceptibility to longer pain and mistakes it puts you in.

Okay, I am stepping off of my cover-up soap box now. Thanks for listening. Back to anger. When it comes to the anger that we feel after losing someone that we love, I have experienced three different areas of anger, which I believe are all important to evaluate when we are in this stage.

1) *We get angry at ourselves.*

My senior year of high school, my hockey team was in the state championship playoffs. We were one win away from the state championship, so close to the thing that we had been working so hard for all year long.

There were only a few minutes left in the game, we were down by one. With time winding down in the game, we took a time out. The play was set. I would get in front of the net, get open, get the pass, and try to score to tie the game. The play unfolded, I got in front of the net, I fought off a defender, got open, got the pass, had the open net, and I missed the net. We lost the game. And it was my fault, all me. Right? I sure thought so.

If you have ever played a sport, or even a game, and you lose, it is super easy to be quick to blame yourself for the loss, right? If you're like me, you think back to ever move that you made, every play that you were a part of, every missed opportunity that you had, and all of the sudden, in your mind, you become the entire reason that your team lost. If only you would have been better, the team would have succeeded. The results would have been different.

When it comes to breakups, in my experience, it is the easiest to get mad at myself. It is so easy to rethink every wrong thing that I did, every conversation that I mismanaged. *Oh, but if I would have just said this... If I would have just done this thing differently... If I would have just been better....* **Would they still be here?**

Maybe the results would look different. Maybe I wouldn't be feeling this pain. It's my fault. Why am I such a screw up?

Ever felt these emotions? Ever feel this anger run through you? Ever understand what being angry with yourself looks like?

It's so easy to pin the blame on ourselves. Why? Because we can have control of it. And if we are honest, we love to have control in whatever we can, especially when it feels like the circumstances around us are so outside of our control. So what do we do? We blame it on ourselves, so that we can control the outcome and deal with the anger. If it is all my fault, then I can confront myself, I can beat myself up for a while, and everything will eventually settle. Then, I'll be okay.

What if there was a better way to be angry? What if it didn't have to lead to bitterness or self-hatred? I believe that it doesn't. You are not the enemy here.

2) *We get angry at the other person.*

I think that in every breakup, this happens, at some point. No matter how well a relationship ended, there will come a point where you get mad at the person who you lost.

Why would they treat me that way? Did they not love me?
How could they leave so easily? Why did they make things so
unhealthy? Did they really unfollow me on Instagram?

It's their fault that it had to end. They are toxic.
Their middle name is red-flag!

I want to validate you for a second. You may be right. A lot of the pain you are feeling may be their fault. Maybe they did screw up in a bad way and your anger is validated.

With that being said, just because your anger is validated, doesn't mean that it is the prison cell that you are called to live in.

Remember the tombs that we talked about in chapter two? The tomb of bitterness is one of the most dangerous tombs to seal ourselves into. Why? Because it is like a revolving door. Anger leads to bitterness and bitterness leads to blindness. The issue with bitterness is that Jesus will give you openings to free you from your tomb, but you won't see them. You will walk through the revolving door of bitterness until you exhaust yourself from trying to break free.

I have a good friend who says it like this: *"Bitterness and unforgiveness is like swallowing poison and expecting it to hurt someone else."*

That's exactly what the bitterness of anger is; Poison. It will slowly creep through your heart and soul until it sneakily shuts down what you need to live the life of freedom that God has for you. Poison kills things.

You ever seen Snow White? If you were deprived from Disney as a kid, let me fill you in. Snow White is a princess and there is this evil queen. See, this evil queen is Snow White's stepmom. Her stepmom's desire is to be the most beautiful person in the land, the fairest of them all. Here's the thing: Snow White's got that beauty card won. The evil queen isn't pumped, so what's she do? She dresses up like an old woman (so creepy, look it up), and she offers Snow White a poisoned apple.

Snow White may have been beautiful, but she wasn't the brightest. Who in the world eats a random apple given to you by some creepy old lady in the woods? Can you say suspicious?

Snow White eats this apple, it's like she didn't learn from Eve. Homegirl needed to read the Gospel. And all of the sudden, she is poisoned and falls into a deep sleep, Disney's way of saying a coma on the way to death.

See if we aren't careful, we will set ourselves up for a Snow White kind of situation. The longer that we allow for bitterness or anger to fester, the more danger we face of the hope, the freedom, and the redemption plan that God has for us falling into a deep sleep, on the verge of death.

But what if there was a way that God wants to allow for you to have anger, but also not allow for it to get to the point of poison? What if there was a healthy way to process anger against the person that you lost? What if it didn't have to lead to the revolving door?

3) *We get angry at God.*

I want to spend some time on this one, as I think it is really important. Getting mad at God can be pretty easy to do, can't it? If God is in control of everything, is all powerful, and is all-knowing, then why wouldn't he do something to help save my relationship? If He really is good all of the time, why doesn't He help my life feel good right now?

This is all His fault.

The blame shifting continues here and the anger follows it. We get mad at God. In my experience with break-ups, anger has looked different in different seasons. What I haven't told you yet is that I have been in two different seasons that have been extremely close to engagement. When the second relationship ended, my anger looked drastically different than the first time.

The first break-up that I went through ended in anger towards the other person. The second? I'll be honest. I was furious with God. I couldn't help but question God and ask why He would give me such confidence that I was living out my redemption story from Him, just to strip it away once again, leaving me in a similar place that I was in a few years before.

My anger was triggered at God like it had never been triggered at Him before. Remember when I said that I am inviting you into my process? Well, in order to process in a real way, it requires vulnerability. So, I am going to be vulnerable with you.

I am a pastor. A lot of times, people can think that this means that I will never question or doubt God. I wish that were true. I wish my faith was so "perfect". That I could always know and believe that God was good and that He wouldn't do anything to hurt me?

Well, that isn't me. I would venture to guess that it isn't any pastor or any believer. I get mad at God. And this time, I was really mad. The questions begin to run through my head:

How could you do this? How can you put me through this? Am I really this unworthy of love? Why do you let all of my friends have awesome marriages and never let me get there? Do you see me as broken?

Our anger with God can begin to misshape the truth, in our minds, of how He sees us and how we see Him. That can be a really dangerous place to live in. Like it or not, the way that we see ourselves shapes the lens that we use to walk through life.

What does that have to do with anger at God? Well let me tell you. My brother… My sister…when you allow for your anger at God to begin to shape the way that you see Him, all of the sudden, the way that you see yourself will begin to deteriorate.

Why? Because whether you realize it or not, God sees you through a perfected filter. You are His daughter, His son. And He loves you through your mess and anger. Your life can be broken, foundation in crumbles, and God still sees you as a child worth dying for. Want to feel some more worth in your life? Check to see if your anger is getting in the way of the filter of God's love for you.

Breakups are hard enough at face value. They have enough confusion and searching behind them. You don't need for your image to be something that is surrounded by confusion and searching too. But this is what anger at ourselves can produce.

The reality is that it's easy to blur the lines of these lenses. So how do you allow yourself to be angry but still maintain the health of allowing God to shape the way you see yourself?

When I was really mad at God, I'll be honest, I had no motivation to reconcile that anger. I wanted to sit in it. I wanted Him to know that I was mad. I wanted Him to feel the cold shoulder that I was giving Him. While my feelings of anger were valid, the only person that I was hurting in these moments was myself.

God is God. He is the Creator of all things. He created emotion. He can take my anger. I can't hurt His feelings. But in moments where I feel like He hasn't treated me fairly, my pride takes over. My walls go up. And I think that the cold shoulder method will work for Him to change my outcome.

So I believe that the first step towards being angry at God, in a healthy way, is to lower the cold shoulder. Get rid of the silent treatment. Use your words. Do not let the anger fester into bitterness, birthed from the silence. Get this: God is trying to speak to you. Did you know that? He wants to answer you. He isn't trying to leave you in silence.

Will there be seasons of intentional silence to allow you to process and seek Him? I believe so. But is He giving you the cold shoulder? Absolutely not. He wants you to hear from Him. But in order to do that, you must be willing to lower your cold shoulder and seek Him. He wants to speak to you through His Word that is living and active.

But I believe that His voice doesn't stop there. He wants to speak to you through the whisper of His Spirit. So often, we expect for God to speak in a mighty and powerful yell, a statement kind of voice. Ever seen *Bruce Almighty*? We expect for God to be like Morgan Freeman, speaking to the point where we can't ignore Him. Isn't it so often that we do ignore God? We allow for the voice of sin, the yell of the craziness of our lives, and our own pride to shield and glaze over the whisper that God is trying to share for us.

In 1 Kings 19:11-12 NLT, Elijah is seeking out the voice of God. I love how His voice is presented.

And as Elijah stood there, the Lord passed by, and a mighty windstorm hit the mountain. It was such a terrible blast that the rocks were torn loose, but the Lord was not in the wind. After the wind there was an earthquake, but the Lord was not in the earthquake. 12 And after the earthquake there was a fire, but the Lord was not in the fire. And after the fire there was the sound of a gentle whisper.

A gentle whisper.

Have you ever played the game telephone? It's a classic children's game where you sit in a circle and the first person comes up with a phrase to pass along to the next person in the circle. Then they tell the other person what they heard and the theme continues until the last person in the circle has a chance to hear what was said. The goal is for the last person to say thing thing that the first person originally said. Usually, what the last person hears is very different than the first person. All of the sudden the phrase "apple sauce and mashed potatoes" can turn into "I want to ride an alligator."

What this game shows is that the more silent the environment around you and the closer you are to the one who is whispering, the more likely you are to hear what is said.

The same theme applies to hearing the whisper
of God: *Silence and Proximity.*

So get alone and get close. I can promise you this: God loves to have quiet moments of intimate silence with you. That doesn't mean you can't be angry. Be angry. Yell at Him, ask questions, tell Him you don't want to talk to Him because it doesn't seem fair. But then, instead of slamming the door and walking away from Him, sit there. Be angry. Be silent. And open your hands and ask Him to speak.

So you're angry? That's okay. You're allowed to be. And I want to reiterate this for a second: Pain sucks. You can be angry at it. You can question it and yell at it. But know this: God's heart for you is to listen, process, and respond. His plan for you is to find your best life. He doesn't promise that the road there won't have pitstops of pain. He doesn't promise that we won't get angry at Him, rooted in our lack of understanding of the end of the road. But what He does promise is to process with us, to walk with us, to love us, and to be a Good Father to us. Be angry, but give room for the Spirit of joy and of peace to make His way into the crevices of that anger.

Just like your pain, your anger is just a season. Don't try to skip past it, but don't let it hold you hostage.

PEACE AND RELEASE

∽

Guatemala is a country that will always have a very special place in my heart. I have spent a collective time of three months in the country on mission. It is an incredible place where I have experienced the presence of God in amazing ways. This isn't a time for one of those stories.

While in Guatemala, we would take a day, every once in a while, where we would do all of the touristy things that Guatemala has. There's a city in Guatemala called Antigua that has tons of markets for tourists to shop at. What some tourists may not know is that it's part of the culture of these markets to negotiate price. This is where I thrive y'all. The more and more times that I would go there, the more and more confident that I would get with my negotiating.

Usually you're negotiating for little souvenirs like pens, soccer jerseys, journals, coffee, machetes, or chocolate. I know, machetes and chocolate. What else could you desire in life?

The majority of Spanish that I know, I learned from my time bargaining with the shop owners. Bargaining became a love language of mine. I lived for the moments that I could walk around the market and try to help the other Americans get the lowest possible prices on their souvenirs.

The thing that I have learned about bargaining is that it has its moments where it is fun, but it also has its moments where it can be the most draining process you can possibly walk through.

Grief Stage 4: **Bargaining**

In terms of bargaining, the grief stage would be the side of bargaining that is classified as draining. It is not enjoyable. Let me ask you... have you ever bargained with someone and felt super drained afterwards? In my experience, when it comes to losing someone you love, it is the season that you may even give the most of your energy towards.

I am a fighter. I want to battle for what I believe in, no matter the cost. Sometimes this is a great attribute about me. But sometimes, like in the bargaining stage of grief, it can be life-draining.

Have you ever seen the movie *Titanic*? It is one of the most famous love stories of all time, and I have to be honest with you: I can't stand it. If you have lived under a rock and haven't ever heard of the Titanic, let me give you my quick version of a recap. The movie is about a massive cruise ship, called the Titanic, that is apparently the safest, most luxurious boat ever created. Spoiler: that's false advertisement.

The most elite of the elite are on this boat. It's like the Queen Elizabeth's and the Beyonce's of their day. Straight royalty. The two main characters are a girl named Rose and a guy named Jack. Jack and Rose have this weird love that kind of makes you a little uncomfortable the whole movie. It is an unlikely love, as Jack is not a crazy wealthy person, like Rose is. It's the classic forbidden love kind-of story.

They have a lot of lovey dovey moments throughout the movie, but this isn't a book about the lovey dovey moments, is it? We are talking about the drowning feeling that comes when something you love has ended, so let's fast forward to that part. The ship hits an iceberg, which is mostly underwater, under the surface. And the ship begins to go down. Through a series of unfortunate events, Jack and Rose end up off of the boat, floating in the freezing cold water. Rose gets to climb up on a piece of floating wood, while Jack is hanging on, treading water, trying to fight to stay afloat.

When our relationship hits the iceberg, the breaking point, and everything under the surface begins to break us down, it can feel like we are treading water, holding on to whatever we can find, trying to stay afloat.

Bargaining is the piece of wood that we hold onto to try to stay afloat. It is the last piece of life that we can see, the last hope for our love to not come to an end. It is looking at the person you love, at God, and at your own mind, in that order, and trying to strike a deal.

When it feels like the person that you love is beginning to pull away, you begin the process of bargaining.

"We can make this work. If you keep fighting with me, things will look different. I can change this thing that you aren't loving about me, I promise. Let's give it a little bit more time. We are just going through a rough patch, let's stay focused on the good moments. We can get counseling. Please don't do this. Give me another chance. Do you know how much I love you? We are so worth fighting for."

The pleas begin to unravel as you feel like you are hanging on by a thread. Bargaining is your "all-in" kind of move and risk, like it would be in poker. The win it all or lose it all kind of mentality. Could it end in the one that you love staying? Maybe. But it also could end in drowning, just like it did for Jack in *The Titanic*.

Can I be honest with you for a second? Bargaining seems like a good option. It seems like one of the only ways that we can still get what we think is best for us. But you deserve more. Your heart deserves more. You deserve to be fought for.

There's a difference between fighting *with* someone for your relationship and bargaining *for* someone to change a mind that has already been made up.

Back to Jack and Rose floating in the Atlantic Ocean after the shipwreck. Isn't it crazy that this is a perfect depiction of what happens when we bargain with the love that we are losing? Rose was floating on top of the piece of wood, safe from the dangers of the water. It doesn't mean that the shipwreck didn't hurt her or affect her life in a drastic way, but she knew she had a good chance of surviving. Meanwhile, Jack was the one in the water, treading water to survive.

Fighting would look like Jack and Rose being together on the piece of wood, fighting for life. Bargaining looks like one of the two drowning, while the other is comfortable with being the only to stay afloat.

Fighting is necessary in all relationships. It won't always look awesome. It won't always be fun. We are each sin-filled people who will constantly fall short and disappoint others. Without fight, no relationship will last. But fighting is different than bargaining. You shouldn't have to convince the one you love to fight and that you are worth fighting for.

We bargain with the person that we love, but we also bargain with God.

See what I think may happen, is that we try to bargain with the one that we love and it doesn't work. So what do we do? We go to God and try to get him to help us change their minds. It's almost like when you were a kid and you asked your mom if you could have a sleepover at a friends house and she said no. So what did you do? You went to your dad and asked again, convinced that he could help you get a different result than the initial one that you were given.

Isn't this kind of how we approach God sometimes?

God, if you would just fix this relationship, I promise to never put you second again. God I know that this is best for me. God, you say that you hear the desires of my heart. I desire this, so can you show the other person that they should desire it too? I'm begging you to change their mind God. You are a God who is good, this is good for me, so will you heal it? Heal it and let the glory go to you.

Am I saying that God can't work in miraculous ways that can change circumstances that seem impossible? Of course not. He is the author of the miraculous. But what I am saying is that there is a certain approach that we should have in this moment that will protect our hearts and accomplish the same mission. How could that be? We will get to that in a second.

Before we do, I want to take a second to dive into the last person that we try to bargain with: Ourselves.

While we bargain within our hearts and minds the entire process, we turn too bargaining with ourselves as a last resort. It is almost denial disguised as bargaining. Our bargaining falls short with the one we love and with God, and the only option we have left is to bargain with our own minds.

This isn't over. If I keep fighting, either the one I love or God will change their mind. They will see my faithfulness and pursuit and will realize that I am the best option for them to be with. I can do this. I can just wait this out.

If you have any experience in bargaining, you know that one of the best tactics that you can have to get the price to where you want it is to walk out, give them time to panic thinking you're gone, and then returning. If you have ever bought a car, then maybe you have tried this. You request a certain price that you want and, if they say no, you bluff and then say something like *"Well I will just take my business elsewhere."* And a lot of the times, the dealership will come down on their price.

When it comes to losing someone that you love, it can be easy to attempt to make your mind believe that this form of bargaining is happening. It isn't really over, it's just an unspoken break that will end with you guys back together. But the reality is that it is probably over, so how do you face the reality that it is and end the bargaining stage?

Through my time of processing and healing, I have discovered a practice that has helped me to hand my bargaining off to God and find freedom every day. Are you ready? It is super simple, yet super effective. Here it is:

In order to find freedom in my healing, I had to intentionally become versed in something I like to call **Peace and Release.**

In order to really explain what this is, there are three elements of this that I need to unpack: *Vent, Peace, and Release.* I know, I know. Vent wasn't in the name of the chapter, but it is what has to happen before we get to the peace or the release part.

Vent. Let God hear it. Cry out the desires of you heart. Don't hold back. Let God know what you want. If you were to have everything go your way, what would it look like? This is your opportunity to not beat around the bush. Tell Him what the perfect deal would look like, where you don't have to bargain anymore. What does your perfect outcome look like?

Venting is really important, but we do not stop there. You cannot stop there because then it is still just you trusting in the your plan, believing that your plan is the only plan that will actually bring you hope or joy. That isn't trust. That isn't relationship with God. That is a conceited view of your circumstances, looking more like a temper-tantrum than a conversation.

Vent to God. Tell Him how you feel. Get it out. But then, it's time to start praying towards peace.

What do I mean by that? We often think that the only way that we will get the peace that we are hoping for is if the one we loved stayed in our life in the role we hoped they would. Here is the problem with that mindset, however: If anything else happens, we feel unease about it. What if God has something better for you? What if His plans, that may be just around the corner, are better than anything you could have ever imagined? So instead of praying towards just the answer you want to hear, you need to pray towards peace.

Peace. Peace is a pretty attractive word, isn't it? This is something that we may hear a lot, but may not be able to tangibly be able to tell you what it feels like. Have you ever heard the line *Peace be with you?* Or how about *Praying for peace for you.*

Those lines are attractive in thought, but finding the application behind them can be a little bit more difficult. But I want for you to hear me when I say this: Even when your life feels more chaotic and confusing than ever before, *peace is still attainable.*

But how? Paul gives us a great step into figuring out the answer to that question in Philippians 4:6-7. He says:

> 6 *Don't worry about anything; instead, pray about every-thing. Tell God what you need, and thank him for all he has done. 7 Then you will experience God's peace, which exceeds anything we can understand. His peace will guard your hearts and minds as you live in Christ Jesus.*

Let's break this down. Don't worry about anything? Okay Paul. That seems a little unreasonable, no? How am I not supposed to worry when it feels like my life has been uprooted? Worry is all I can think to do right now. My future seems so uncertain now. Have you been here? Are you here right now? Thinking, yea Paul, that would be great bro, but worrying may as well be my profession at this point.

I don't think that Paul is simply saying "Hey, just stop worrying." That feels unrealistic and like some pretty bad advice. See what I think he could actually be saying is that we need to allow for our worry to come out of the depths of our minds and hearts and into the hands of the One who can do something with it. Worry isn't always a bad thing. It can be a motivating force to get us to do things that we need to do. For example, to be worried about getting to school or work on time is a healthy worry. You set your alarm to make sure that you don't wake up late, you have clean clothes, you make sure to get your coffee and some breakfast, you make sure there is gas in your car, things like that.

You do these things because there is something in you that is slightly worried about being late for work or school, so you have preceding actions to avoid allowing for that worry to come to fruition.

Not all worry is bad. The issue is that we allow for the worry that is bad to stay internalized or we bring it to the wrong outlets.

Have you ever been to Europe? Well if you haven't, you need to go. Every country that I have been to within Europe has been amazing. Here's a word of advice: when you go, make sure to prepare for the things that are different than the United States. I did not do this. And guess what is different...the outlets. Phone, watch, computer, airpods, all needing outlets. These European outlets were like massive holes in the wall. They were nothing close to the outlet I thought I'd have available. For American chargers, you need the right outlet adapter to be able to give energy back to your devices. If you don't adapt to the necessary outlet, the battery on your devices will continue to drain until they have nothing left.

Trying to outlet our worry to any source but God is like trying to plug an American charger into a European outlet. It is useless and will just continue to drain your battery until there is nothing left.

So what is the outlet? Paul shows us, right after talking about worry. He says to *pray about everything.* How do you pray about everything?

Let me debunk a prayer myth for you. Prayer is not just for "prayer moments". It's not just for before meals, before bed, or before a big moment in your life. Praying about everything means praying at all times. It means to talk to God like you talk to yourself.

Maybe I am just a weird guy, but I definitely talk to myself all of the time. It's not always out loud, but I talk to myself a lot in my head. I'll talk to myself walking through the grocery store, in my drives to work, while I'm doing the dishes, on my runs, sitting at coffee shops, in my bed at nights, in the shower in the mornings, and many other moments. If we can be honest with ourselves, we are pretty vocal with ourselves.

Could you imagine what would happen if we turned that self-dialogue to God-dialogue? Back to what Paul is writing in Philippians. He isn't saying to not worry. What I think he is saying is that if we would just turn our own thoughts of worry into a consistent dialogue with God, worry would be replaced with peace in ways we can't even understand.

Paul is saying that if we just have a constant dialogue of asking God what we need and thanking Him for what we have, the direct result is peace. Isn't it crazy that we serve a God that is so good that He creates space for peace that is attainable, regardless of the external circumstances that are happening around us?

And what does this peace do? It's crazy because it doesn't just calm our minds and let us get better sleep at night. The promise that God gives us is that His peace will guard our hearts and our minds. Your heart has the potential to be guarded from further hurt. It doesn't mean that your pain disappears, but it means that God will help to keep you there and give you peace as you heal.

Peace is available to you, my friend. Not just in the future, but today. What's the special ingredient? Living in Christ Jesus. Releasing your agendas. Having constant communication with God. Heal in the peace that surpasses your own understanding. Stop the negotiation. Make the peace and release method a daily rhythm in your life.

NO MORE WHITE FLAGS

T hree o'clock in the morning. Awakened from the light sleep that you fought so hard to distract your mind long enough to fall into. Eyes remained closed because you are hoping that you waking up once again is just a bad dream. Tossing and turning, realizing you have at least three or four more hours until you can wake up. You feel restless. This is when the battle ground comes to life. The war inside has begun.

Have you ever seen the movie *Inside Out*? I've only seen it in Spanish. And as I mentioned in the last chapter, my Spanish is only good for negotiation, so my understanding of the movie is pretty much what I can see at face value. There are all of these animated characters, who each represent an emotion. The emotions that are presented are Joy, Sadness, Fear, Anger and Disgust, and they are all running around in the mind of a teenage girl. Working in student ministry for so long, I can tell you that the mind of a teenage girl is a wild place to run around in.

In the middle of the mind, there is a control board, where the emotions each stand to navigate what the girl is feeling. Throughout the movie, the emotions argue over who controls what, within certain scenarios that the girl walks through. At one point in the movie, the teenage girl moves to a new city and feels like everything that she knows has been stripped from her. All of the sudden, Joy, who used to conquer a majority of the girl's thoughts, falls to the back burner and Sadness, Fear, Anger, and Disgust seem to take over.

Isn't this such a true representation for how our minds can work? It can feel like joy has to work so hard to keep its voice in the midst of the influence of fear, sadness, anger, and disgust. It feels like joy is on its own sometimes, within a sea of negativity.

Back to three in the morning. It feels like joy has been squashed by sadness and fear. The war inside has started strong, yet it feels like you are already losing.

If you grew up in church, or have ever been to Sunday school, you have probably heard of a story of some guys named David and Goliath. If you haven't, let me take a second to catch you up to speed.

This is the "STV" version of the story, in other words, the "Sean Translated Version" of it. So basically the story starts out, in 1 Samuel 17, when a war breaks out between the Israelites and the Philistines. And a lot is on the line in this war. The winner has victory and territory. The loser has to become the slaves of the winners. So, of course, each side would want to send out their absolute best to fight and represent their nation.

The Philistines show their cards first, and in terms of poker, they have a royal flush. They send out a man named Goliath to represent them and fight for their freedom. This behemoth of a man rolls out onto the battlefield and begins taunting the Israelites. Keep in mind, Goliath is over nine feet tall. He has full armor and a massive spear, with the tip of the spear weighing 15 pounds…

If you have ever dropped a 15 pound weight on your toe, you know the pain it can cause, and now multiply that by a nine foot man in armor throwing it at you. It's no joke. So, naturally, the Israelites saw Goliath standing on the battlefield and were terrified. They had no nine feet men to send out to face him, so what did they do? They sat still, trapped in their fear.

When the war inside has been initiated, that is often where you will find yourself living: trapped in fear, trying to avoid what is waiting for you in the middle of the battlefield.

Fear is crippling. Fear can lead to self-deprecation, complacency, and depression.

Grief Stage 5: **Depression and Loneliness**

Can we pause for a second and talk about depression?

Can we talk about how real it is?

Depression is no joke. It shifts your personality, your desires, your day to day, and the way you see yourself, see others and see God. When you are facing the war inside, and grieving the loss of someone you loved, depression can be a stage of grief that can feel like it lasts a lifetime. Depression is a slippery slope.

You don't enjoy things you once loved. Nothing can make you happy. It's your fault you're depressed. You should just snap out of it, right? It feels like your mind has given up on you. You can't eat. You can't sleep. You feel like you barely can live. Life just may not seem worth living. You wake up with a black cloud over your head and every time that the sun starts to shine through the darkness, it turns to lightning and thunder, with rain so hard you can't help but stay down and try to find shelter anywhere you can. Joy? What's that? All you know are the moments that suck a little bit less than moments before then.

When you battle depression and add in the pain of someone you love leaving, it can become easy to think you are easily forgotten. You'll never be picked or chosen first. You aren't wanted. You may even deserve to be abandoned, right? Because you aren't good enough. You don't deserve value, worth, love, time, or freedom to move forward.

When you see depression in the middle of the battlefield, the war may seem impossible to win.

Depression is a constant internal war that you feel like you have to wake up every day and fight, believing in your mind that there is no way to find victory.

The Israelites believed that there was no way that they could find victory. They didn't know where to turn next. They stood trapped in fear, on the brink of surrender, terrified of accepting the coming slavery to the Philistines, which had to seem unavoidable.

And then a shepherd boy, David, wandered onto the scene of fear, simply to bring the army food and resources. The Israelite army viewed this boy as inadequate and unequipped to stand with the rest of the troops, nonetheless go to battle with the behemoth Goliath. But David feels a stirring within him and he believes he can conquer Goliath. And so he goes up to King Saul. To him, it is time to let this shepherd boy go to battle. But the reaction isn't quite as David would have originally hoped that it would be. Check it out:

> 32 *"Don't worry about this Philistine," David told Saul. "I'll go fight him!"*

> 33 *"Don't be ridiculous!" Saul replied. "There's no way you can fight this Philistine and possibly win! You're only a boy, and he's been a man of war since his youth."*

You are only a boy. You are only a girl. You have never conquered this before. You are not strong enough. You are not worthy enough. You can't do it.

The Goliath that you are battling has been defeating victims since before you ever knew him. What makes you think that you can actually conquer this? Go back into fear. Go back into hiding. It is less dangerous.

Aren't these the thoughts that can quickly flood our minds and hearts? When staring down the Goliath of depression, especially after heartbreak, we can often listen to the thoughts that the King Saul's in our minds feed us: that we aren't strong enough to get past it and that the battle isn't worth fighting. Those thoughts can become extremely draining and toxic to the healing that the Lord is trying to help for us to reach.

> *34 But David persisted. "I have been taking care of my father's sheep and goats," he said. "When a lion or a bear comes to steal a lamb from the flock, 35 I go after it with a club and rescue the lamb from its mouth. If the animal turns on me, I catch it by the jaw and club it to death. 36 I have done this to both lions and bears, and I'll do it to this pagan Philistine, too, for he has defied the armies of the living God! 37 The Lord who rescued me from the claws of the lion and the bear will rescue me from this Philistine!"*
>
> *Saul finally consented. "All right, go ahead," he said. "And may the Lord be with you!"*

I think that there are a few different things that we can learn from David, in this moment, that can help us with our approach to the Goliath that we are going to go to war with.

David persisted. The definition of persisted is to go on stubbornly in spite of opposition. So let me ask you, in your life, your circumstances, your heartache…

What would it look like for you to go on stubbornly in spite of the opposition that you face?

When your massive Goliath is standing in front of you, doing its best to leave you stuck stranded in fear, what would it look like for you to persist? Here is the reality of what our Goliaths are going to try to do: make you believe that you are too weak for the battlefield. You belong in the fields, far away from the battle. Just like King Saul did, this may even happen with those who are fighting with you. But what if you could persist?

Persisting looks like seeking counseling to heal, when every voice inside of you says to hide your pain and not let it show. To persist looks like continuing to read the Bible and to pray, even when the will of God doesn't make sense in the moment. To persist looks like trying to find forgiveness for the person who hurt you, even though it would be easy to stay stuck in bitterness. To persist looks like stubbornly doing whatever it takes to come face-to-face with your Goliath on the battleground.

Because David persisted, he was able to go to the battlefield and face Goliath head on. But before he walked out on the battlefield, King Saul, the terrified leader on the sidelines, wanted to equip him to fight Goliath.

> *38 Then Saul gave David his own armor—a bronze helmet and a coat of mail. 39 David put it on, strapped the sword over it, and took a step or two to see what it was like, for he had never worn such things before.*
>
> *"I can't go in these," he protested to Saul. "I'm not used to them." So David took them off again. 40 He picked up five smooth stones from a stream and put them into his shepherd's bag. Then, armed only with his shepherd's staff and sling, he started across the valley to fight the Philistine.*

Saul tries to give David armor and a sword to go to battle with. But he declines the offer. Can you imagine what the other soldiers must have been thinking? "This man is really about to try to fight a nine foot Goliath with a staff and a slingshot...stupid shepherd boy. He has no idea how to be at war. We are going to lose. This boy stands no chance. We stand no chance at victory."

I imagine that David had an extreme silent confidence about him. He walked with a swagger. I don't think that he just walked out on to that battlefield. I imagine that it was more of a strut. He just came from tending sheep in a field to saying "put me in coach" to King Saul to denying the king's armor and sword and choosing a slingshot instead. He was ready to go. He was ready for war.

The beautiful thing about knowing the goodness and the faithfulness of God is that we can always walk with a silent confidence. No matter what we are walking into, we can strut with a swagger. Because there is no war that the mighty power of God is not ready for. And He will always provide us with the tools that we need to battle.

Goliath thought it was hilarious that a young boy was about to fight him, with Israel's freedom on the line, with no armor and a slingshot. He mocked him:

> *41 Goliath walked out toward David with his shield bearer ahead of him, 42 sneering in contempt at this ruddy-faced boy. 43 "Am I a dog," he roared at David, "that you come at me with a stick?" And he cursed David by the names of his gods. 44 "Come over here, and I'll give your flesh to the birds and wild animals!" Goliath yelled.*

But no words were going to be able to touch the swagger that David was walking with. Goliath thought that he had the victory in the bag, easy dubs. But what Goliath didn't account for was the power that comes when someone walks in the promises and the power of God. David was walking in the power of God and the promises of His faithfulness and His victory.

The enemy believes that he has this battle against you in the bag. He thinks that you are the major underdog, with no hopes of a comeback. Can I remind you that your enemy, Satan, hates you? He waits to attack and penetrate every one of your weaknesses. He wants you to fail. He will do everything in his power to deceive you and cause you to be paralyzed by your fear and your insecurities. He will do everything in his power to make depression the way that you identify yourself, not only the season you may be walking through. Satan's goal for your life is very clear: to kill, to steal, and to destroy. As you go into every battle in life, your enemy will do everything he can to kill your drive, steal your confidence, and destroy your worth. And that is where the battle begins.

David wasn't shaken by the schemes of the enemy. He was ready for the fight ahead of him. Why? Because he knew the power that went before him, lived with him, and guided his every step. Goliath may have had better visible armor and weapons, but David had the leader of the greatest army, Heaven's Army, on his side. And so David walked into battle, knowing that victory would be the result:

> *45 David replied to the Philistine, "You come to me with sword, spear, and javelin, but I come to you in the name of the Lord of Heaven's Armies—the God of the armies of Israel, whom you have defied. 46 Today the Lord will conquer you, and I will kill you and cut off your head. And then I will give the dead bodies of your men to the birds and wild animals, and the whole world will know that there is a God in Israel! 47 And everyone assembled here will know that the Lord rescues his people, but not with sword and spear. This is the Lord's battle, and he will give you to us!"*

There is a specific line that I want for us to focus on in what David just said here:

Today the Lord will conquer you, and I will kill you.

David is approaching Goliath and talking up a big game. But notice what he says: Today the **Lord** *will* conquer you. He didn't say that today will be the day that I will conquer you. This statement shows the power that comes from the faith that the Lord will do it. Let me ask you: Do you believe that the Lord will conquer the battle that you are in right now? More importantly, have you surrendered the battle, fully, to the hand of the Lord?

Don't miss this. The reason that David was successful in, what seemed to be, an impossible battle, is because he fully surrendered the battle to the Lord before he even stepped foot on the battle field.

A lot of the times, to surrender feels like the opposite of victory, right? I have watched enough Looney Toon cartoons growing up to know that a white flag means to surrender, and when the white flag is waved, the battle is over. The process of surrendering is admitting defeat, right? That seems to be the mindset that many of us have grown up believing. To surrender means to give up on the fight. To surrender means to admit weakness, and that is the opposite of what we should do. To surrender means that you don't care about winning anymore.

Can I redefine this word, *surrender*, for a minute? Because here's what I believe: if we want to win the battle that Satan is trying to win against us, we have to understand the power of surrender.

No more white flags. It's time to battle. But in a battle, don't you long to have the strongest power on your side? This is the power that we have access to through surrendering to the Father. Paul reminds us of this, in Ephesians 1:19-20:

"What is the immeasurable greatness of his power toward us who believe, according to the working of his great might that he worked in Christ when he raised him from the dead and seated him at his right hand in the heavenly places".

Do you understand what Paul is saying to us here?! We have the ability to access the power that rose Christ from the grave, in our every day battles. Think about that. There is an available, miraculous power that rose a dead man back to life, available for your use! But to access it, we have to surrender our own strength to the power that faith in Jesus brings. Scripture is clear. In our weakness, we are made strong.

I love the way that Eugene Peterson words this, in The Message translation of the Bible. It proclaims:

"My grace is enough; it's all you need. My strength comes into its own in your weakness. Once I heard that, I was glad to let it happen. I quit focusing on the handicap and began appreciating the gift. It was a case of Christ's strength moving in on my weakness. Now I take limitations in stride, and with good cheer, these limitations that cut me down to size—abuse, accidents, opposition, bad breaks. I just let Christ take over! And so the weaker I get, the stronger I become."

The answer is Jesus. In what other place does your weakness equate to the greatest strength imaginable? In what other place does someone say: *Hey, it's okay. Sit in your weakness, I will use it to make you victorious.*

You may be thinking: *Sean… David wasn't weak. He didn't just have his heart broken. He wasn't trapped in depression. Like sure, Goliath may have been physically stronger than him, but mentally, there's no way that he was as weak as I am right now. He had the words to say to Goliath. I can't even think of words to get myself through my day, everyday. David was confident. I could not be more insecure inside right now. David believed in himself. I pretty firmly believe that I am a worthless failure right now. How could you compare us? How do you think that I could actually defeat the Goliath of heartache?*

David also had moments of insecurity. He had moments of seeing himself as a failure. He had moments of bad mental health. It's all throughout the Psalms.

But in this moment, maybe David had more confidence and mental strength than you do right now. But, my friend, can I ask you a question? Could it be that David had that confidence because it wasn't the

IF YOU LOVE SOMEONE....

first time that he had to channel the inner-strength that comes in the power of Jesus?

I mean, think about the life of David for a second. This was not his first battle. David was first a shepherd, which, if you didn't know, is the job that is usually given to the child who is viewed to have the least potential of the family. So, from a young age, David had to overcome the stigma and insecurities that would have come and being seen, by his own father, as the least likely to amount to anything in life. How did he do that? He leaned on the power of God.

His need for God's power continued. This is the same man who had to fight off lions and bears to protect his sheep. Do you not think he had to rely on the power of God in those moments too? I don't know about you, but I have been to a zoo. And let me tell you, there ain't no way that I'm saving a sheep from the mouth of a lion or a bear on my strength!

And now, David is up against 9'3" Goliath and he is so confident, that he not only says he will win, he says he will cut off his head. Why is he confident? Because over and over and over and over again in David's life, he surrenders his battles to the Lord and acknowledges that they are the Lord's battles. Over and over, he is excited to surrender his own strength and his own plans because he knows that his God will always deliver.

So often, in the battle ground of heartbreak and the battle of depression, we can struggle to believe that God will deliver. With the relationship just ending, it seems like He just failed us. You so desperately want to not be depressed anymore, but everyday it remains where you are. So why in the world would you trust He is going to deliver? This is where we must remind ourselves of God's faithfulness.

I would venture to guess this isn't the first time that you have been disappointed in your life. I would venture to guess there have been other times where you have felt like God didn't come through for you. But... I would also venture to guess that in every disappointment, there has been a breakthrough that you could have never seen coming in the moment that the disappointment hit. I would venture to guess that maybe, just maybe, God has continuously come through in your past, when you never thought it would be possible.

So, could it be possible that He will come through once again? See, David was mentally confident, in a place where there was no reason to be, because he knew that the Lord's power thrived in circumstances that seemed impossible.

What if you believed that the Lord's power would thrive most in the most impossible situations in your life? And all you had to do was surrender and let Him run the show. Again, *This is the Lord's battle*, not yours, to fight.

As David approached Goliath on the battlefield, he didn't hesitate. He didn't throw a white flag. He charged in, knowing the battle was already won. A slingshot and a stone...two simple tools that David partnered with the Lord's power, and the battle had been won.

To any normal human being, a slingshot and a stone feel like useless tools in a battle of this magnitude. But the Lord uses these simple tools to defeat the greatest of enemies. They just had to be utilized within the context of the power of God, in His plan, in His timing, stemming from the surrender of David.

Can I blow your mind for a second?

We always say prayers like:

God, would you get me out of this battle?

God, give me what I need to win this.

God, give me the power to get through this.

God, I don't have what I need to beat this. I can't do it.

    Can you help me?

But here's what I believe for you: You probably already possess the tools that you need to win your battle against your Goliath. You may be waiting for God to come through and supernaturally reveal some divine tools that you have never seen before to give you victory in your battle. Could it just be possible that you haven't tried partnering them with the power of the Lord? Maybe your prayer needs to simply shift from *God, give me the tools* to *God, reveal to me what tools that I possess that I need to partner with your power today.* And then surrender and allow the Lord to use your simple tools to be powerful weapons of victory. This is exactly what happened with the simple tools of David, matched with the power of the Lord:

> *48 As Goliath moved closer to attack, David quickly ran out to meet him. 49 Reaching into his shepherd's bag and taking out a stone, he hurled it with his sling and hit the Philistine in the forehead. The stone sank in, and Goliath stumbled and fell face down on the ground. 50 So David triumphed over the Philistine with only a sling and a stone, for he had no sword. 51 Then David ran over and pulled Goliath's sword from its sheath. David used it to kill him and cut off his head.*

He triumphed...with **only** a sling and a stone. How? Because in his battle, he surrendered to the power of the Lord and let Him fight the battle, because David knew that in the power of the Lord, there is victory.

I love how this battle ends. David uses Goliath's weapon against him to cut off his head. Friend, I know that in the battle of depression, you are constantly hearing thoughts and lies about your identity, your worth, your purpose, and your strength. It's like a broken record. But let me speak this truth over your life today: If you surrender to the power of the Lord, and let Him guide your fight in your battle, He will not only lead you to victory over the Goliath of depression, He will teach you how to use the enemies lies and deceits for your advantage. What do I mean?

When, (yes I said when), the Lord brings victory to the battle of depression and the battle of heartbreak, that you are walking through right now, He will help you to turn those lies into truth. In the battle, the lies of Satan push you further from Jesus and the hope that He brings. But, when you allow Jesus to begin to rewire the way that you think, you will start to see those lies you once believed, as just that, lies. And the truth of the Word of God will teach you to identify the schemes of Satan as pitiful attempts to back you down from the victory that Jesus has already won for you. In the truth of the Lord, you will be able to use the lies and schemes of the enemy to cut off his head, because you know where your truth and your hope lies: in the name of Jesus.

Hear me on this: Depression is very real. It is no joke. There are some people who have physiological reasons, traumatic reasons, or biological links to depression that require medicine and counseling. It's very real.

But also, hear me on this: Your Savior, Jesus, is very real too. And His victorious power has the strength to win any battle, any Goliath, and any lie that stands against you.

Do you believe it?

SMASH THE REAR VIEWS

∽

Golf is not my sport.

I find it to be one of the most frustrating things that this world has to offer, and I consider myself to be a pretty athletic human being. Growing up, I played baseball, basketball, lacrosse, tennis, and hockey. I played hockey in college, and I still play tennis and hockey on a weekly basis. I know that I am pretty athletic. But golf? Golf defies the concept of athleticism. Golf is its own universe. And every time I play it, everything that I think I know about sports goes out of the window.

If you've ever seen the movie *Happy Gilmore*, I thought that I had hope. Being a hockey player, Adam Sandler made it seem like I would be able to go pro quick. All I had to do was run up to the ball as I drove it and buy a putter that looked like a hockey stick. Easy. Problem solved. So I went online and found a hockey stick putter (yes, it is awesome). And I went out to the golf course, expecting to play like Happy did to beat Shooter McGavin. (If you haven't watched the movie, do yourself a favor and check it out).

As I stepped up to the tee to drive the ball, I had all of the confidence in the world. I took a few steps back, said a quick prayer, and ran to hit the ball, expecting to drive it 400 yards. I ran up, I swung as hard as I could, I missed the ball completely, and I fell.

Shame and remorse. These were the thoughts that instantly ran through my veins as I heard the laughter of my friends behind me. It didn't go as expected. I made some decisions that I thought would benefit my game, but they really only made it worse. In that moment, I knew that I had to have taken the wrong approach.

Grief Stage 6: **Remorse**

When we lose someone that we love, it can feel like we just took the wrong approach, can't it? Our minds constantly look back at all of things that we may have done wrong. And quickly, we get stuck in the trap of the *"if only's"*.

If only I chose different words in that moment...

If only I had pursued them better in that season...

If only I had prioritized them here...

If only that outside circumstance had been different...

If only I handled stress better...

If only I would have fought harder instead of leaving...

If only I kept my cool more...

If only I handled this differently...

If only I took a different approach...

If only, if only, if only. And in these if only's, we are led to a place where we begin to believe "if only ____ was different, I would have never lost them". This is called remorse. Remorse is the sadness or the regret you get from looking back at a situation that could have gone differently. In my experience, this has been the hardest of the stages of grief and healing to shake. As the *if only's* continue to form, it gets harder because we often will get a desire to reach out to the person and ask them if things would be different if we did that thing differently. But most times, we can't reach out because we know reaching out will only make it worse.

So we become stuck. A swirling storm of shame, regret, insecurity, and remorse turn our day dreams to nightmares, as we struggle to believe that the relationship was actually supposed to end. Let me ask you: Have you ever allowed for your thoughts to get to a place where you can actually believe that maybe, just maybe, that relationship was supposed to come to an end?

As someone who is on the other end of more than one heartbreak, I can empathize with you and say that I totally get that right now it may be feel like everything is your fault. It may feel like if you would have just done something different, then that person would have seen you as worth fighting for. It may feel like you are a mess up. You can't do anything right and you always mess up a good thing. I have been there. I have believed those thoughts. I have allowed for those things to shape the way that I looked at myself and understood my worth.

But as someone who has been through the stages of grief and has had to walk through some hard healing, I would love to also pose a question to you:

Could it be that by ending what you had, God is saving you from future hurt?

For so long after the one that I loved left, I blamed God. I was mad at God. Why would you let me walk through this? Why do I have to feel all of this hurt again? It didn't make sense to me. I couldn't comprehend it. I didn't get why fighting for her didn't work. I didn't get why there were so many unanswered questions. I kept looking back and reliving and trying to swim upstream in a river that wasn't meant to be swam in.

I got caught staring in the rear views. To be honest with you, I got caught believing that if I could only recapture the relationship I was in, I could recapture my life. If I could redo some of my "if only's", I could recapture my joy and get back on track with my plan.

But what I realized, is that I had it completely backwards. I was trapped in the rear views while God's desire for me was to see what He was navigating me to. When you are driving a vehicle and look in the rearview mirror, it can be good for a second. It can help you see where you have been, who is behind you, and if there are any potential dangers coming.

But what happens when you get caught looking at the rearview for too long? You lose sight of what is in front of you. Your car can start to swerve, and you are in danger of crashing into something that will hurt you and other people. No person with any driving skills would look at the rearview mirror for that long, right? Because we know that it would put our lives in danger.

So why is it that we treat the rearview mirrors of relationships differently?

When something we loved ends, all we focus on is the rearview mirrors. We treat rearview mirrors like a time machine, don't we? The longer that we look at it, the more likely we feel like it will bring us back there. We think that if we live in memories and stay seated in remorse, our lives can stay in where we have been instead of having to actually move on and look forward.

Why do we live in remorse? Why do we get caught in the rearview? See, I believe that it could be that we have an internal belief and fear that what is in the future will not be as good as what was in the past. We get caught believing that because our plan didn't go accordingly, there is no way to get it back. Instead, we are destined for hurt and for disappointment. But can I save you from some pain that I had to walk through? Don't believe that lie.

You may believe that by losing that person, God snatched you from fulfillment and sent you down a path of pain. But you have it backwards. God isn't in the business of taking away life, He's in the business of creating new life. I pray that you would be able to believe today that by ending what you were in, God is saving you from pain and driving you towards true life.

I don't know about you, but when I get upset or mad, sometimes I just have a desire to smash some things. After my first really hard breakup, I attempted to take up boxing. While I never got into the sparring that came with boxing, I went to the gym multiple times a week to just smash the heavy bags as hard as I possibly could. It released stress and cleared my mind in a really hard season.

There are literally companies that create "rage rooms", where you can pay to come and smash anything from plates to TV's to car windows. I went to one of them one time and the packages that you purchased were literally called "*smash* packages". Why do they make money? Because the creator of these companies know that sometimes, in order to move on from pain and hurt, certain things need to be smashed. The same is true for us when we are stuck in constant remorse.

It's time to **smash the rear view mirrors.**

No more getting stuck on them. No more *if only's*. No more what if's. No more chaining ourselves down to the past, believing that it is the only way that leads back to joy and the life we are desiring. No more believing that person is your purpose. No more thinking they were the only one for you. It's time to smash those thoughts in the face and move on to your true purpose: The future God is laying in front of you.

We need to reset our eyes, minds, and hearts and see where God is leading is. Satan uses remorse to distract you from hope. He knows that as long as you have your eyes set on what could have been, you will continue to miss out on what will be, if you heal.

So, how do we practically smash the rear views?

1) Remember God's faithfulness.

In the moment of heartbreak and hurt, it can feel like God is no-where to be found. He can feel absent, like He has abandoned you, like His plan for you is hurt, like He is in hiding, and like He is silent. These are the moments when it is easiest to doubt that He loves you the way that He says that He does in Scripture, right?

I mean let's be honest for a second. I know that a typical church answer or small group answer would be something like "Yea, it's hard but God's with me". But so often, inside, we feel like He is nowhere to be found. It feels like He has abandoned us.

Listen, I am a pastor. And I have believed these thoughts in the past. You are not alone in thinking these things and believing that God is nowhere to be found. But, as someone who has been stuck, hopeless, believing these things about God, I want to encourage you and challenge you with what helped me break out of that toxic thought pattern.

The direct antidote to counteract the poison that is believing God isn't for you is remembering His faithfulness for you. What do I mean by that? Even in the moments when it seems hardest to see how close Jesus is, there is still a way to know of his nearness. There is still a way to be reminded of His presence.

In the Bible, the nation of Israel continually ran from God. They created and worshipped other idols. They chose their own plans. They sinned against Him. But the beauty of the Gospel shows that even when they ran, God pursued them. Even when they were faithless, God was faithful. He spoke to them and reassured them. But then, at the end of the Old Testament, there came a point where He didn't. He went silent...for 400 years.

I'm an extrovert on steroids. Most other extroverts feel introverted to me because of how extroverted I am. Because of this, I HATE silence.

Have you ever seen the movie *A Quiet Place*? It an incredible, suspenseful movie that has a unique twist. Pretty much the entire movie is in silence, because if noise is made, the monster in the movie will find them and kill them. And let me tell you... I have never been so stressed in a movie in my entire life. Not because of what was happening, but because of what wasn't happening. It was a hour and half hours of silence. No talking. And all I desired was for the silence to break.

When we go through a breakup, we hate silence. Silence from the person we just lost, silence from friends we used to have, silence from family who don't know what to say, and, most of all, silence from God.

But you think not hearing from God for a few months is hard? Imagine 400 years! For 400 years, God revealed nothing new to His people. He didn't speak. He didn't move. And it felt like Israel was left on their own.

Does this sound familiar to you right now?

Does it feel like God is silent, like He disappeared?

I want to offer a different perspective to this story. At face value, it can definitely feel as though God abandoned the nation of Israel for 400 years. But what if His silence was on purpose, with the purpose for us to recapture our perspective?

What if He didn't ditch the nation of Israel, but instead knew that He had already given them all that they needed to find the hope and life that they longed for. All they had to do was remember God's faithfulness.

Over and over again, He has been faithful:

Covering Eve with sacrifice in the Garden of Eden (Genesis 3)

Providing a ram for Abraham to sacrifice instead of Isaac (Genesis 22)

Bringing Joseph from prison to a ruler over Egypt (Genesis 41)

Delivering Israel out of slavery and parting the Red Sea (Exodus 14)

Giving the nation of Israel a promised land to return to (Joshua 1)

Promising a Savior to rescue them from their sin (Isaiah 7)

These are just a few examples of the many moments of the faithfulness of God. These are stories and instances of God continually saying *"Regardless of your mistakes and all of the times that you have turned away from me, I will still make a way for you"*.

He may have felt silent to the nation of Israel, but once again, He was actually just preparing another way for Him to demonstrate His faithfulness. At the end of the 400 years, The Savior, Jesus, came onto the scene. And the world has never been the same.

While many within the nation of Israel may have seen the silence of God as absence, what if they could have shifted their perspective to expectancy for Him to come through?

I have learned the way that I need to approach seasons of silence. When I feel like the line of communication has gone silent between myself and God, I need to believe in expectancy instead of submit to a false narrative of disappointment.

Can you relate to this? Listen. I know silence is scary. It's intimidating. It's uncertain. It can feel suspenseful. And when you lose the person that you love, it can be very easy to find yourself in a world of disappointment, where the Father, that you so desperately need to speak, can feel completely silent. And the voices of everything else in life can begin to be the only voices that you hear.

The voice of self-empowerment culture will tell you that emotion is weakness and to shove it down and move on. The voice of temptation will tell you that a drink or two is the perfect medicine to forget. The voice of culture will tell you that you need to find strength by putting yourself back out there and to hook up with someone else so the pain will go away. The voice of the enemy will tell you that you will be lonely forever and that your God did this and He doesn't care about you.

Silence will do its best to take you out. But if you can remember the faithfulness of God and believe that He is making a way to life for you, the silence will be worth every moment.

The nation of Israel was given the Messiah, Jesus Christ. The awaited bridge needed for perfect relationship with their perfect Heavenly Father happened! And if he brought Jesus, the literal source of eternal life, at the end of Israel's season of silence, what kind of life could God be preparing for you at the end of your season of silence?

Friend, your God is a God of faithfulness. He is faithful to deliver and faithful to bring life to the most dead of situations. You can smash the rearview mirrors by having faith in the destination of life that God is bringing you towards.

2) Remind ourselves of what is good.

Do you know what rearview mirrors are really good at? Making it seem like the prime of your life is in the past. It's behind you. You've passed it. You missed the exit towards happiness and fulfillment and now you feel lost, in the middle of nowhere. When we are stuck looking at where have been, we can often get stuck believing that our life is just bad. The enemy will do whatever he can to keep us there. Isn't it so true that every moment we believe that life is bad, it deflates the hope that anyone else tries to instill in us?

So, what if we could remind ourselves of what is good? And you may be thinking *"Yea okay...because it's that easy?"* Well it may not be easy to not see your situation as bad. The reality is that it might be bad. That heartbreak may be bad. The loss of circles of friends may be bad. The awkwardness that can come with navigating the aftermath of a relationship may have some bad elements.

But hear me. Just because a situation is awful, doesn't mean this season of your life has to be awful. So, how do we regain what is good? We need to take back our perspective.

Perspective changes everything. It can help you find good that you can hold onto in the seasons that feel bad. Let me show you. Let's go through some of the rear views that can be really hard to stop looking at. Then, let's see how we can shift the perspective.

Stuck in the rearview: *Now that they are out of my life, my life will be less fun and my weekends will be lonely.*

Shifted perspective: *I am going to use my newfound free time to reconnect and dive deeper in friendships, dive into Scripture and learn who Jesus is and who He says I am, and find new hobbies that bring me life and purpose.*

Stuck in the rearview: *I found joy in them, purpose in them, life in them. They were my other half.*

Shifted perspective: *My purpose had limits because it was dependent of another person. My purpose can now be limitless because I can redefine my purpose and rediscover it in the limitless potential of life in Jesus. And even in my next relationship, my purpose will remain in the limitless Jesus.*

Stuck in the rearview: *I am unworthy of love. I am done with dating. If that didn't work out, how can I expect anything to? I just ruin it. I'll just send up back here.*

Shifted perspective: *There is a reason that this didn't work out. The next relationship will not be the same because the person and season of life isn't the same. I won't be the same. I will grow and heal by then. Yes, I need time and space to heal, but I know God will bring to me into a better relationship in the future.*

Can you see what happens when we shift our perspectives? Now, I know this is easier said than done. It requires repetition. The lies of the rearview will cycle on repeat. They will feel like relentless thoughts. What I am urging you to do is to cycle these shifted perspectives on repeat just as much, if not more, than the lies of the rearview. This will develop healthy thought patterns in your minds that will begin to bring freedom and hope for the future.

We can remind ourselves of what is good because our situation doesn't define goodness. Our hope defines goodness. And good news! Our hope is in a good God who wants good for us.

Regardless of how bad the season or situation in life may seem, there is always good because there is always God. And we need to run to that hope.

NEW WINE

⌒∕⌒

When you go through heartbreak, in my experience, they're a lot of moments that feel very blurry to remember. I can't look back and tell you every prayer that I ever prayed. I can't think back to every tear I cried. I can't recollect every conversation I had with friends and mentors. There are many days, weeks, even months, that just feel like a blur.

But then there are specific moments, in the midst of the internal chaos, that I feel like God allows us to remember. As I think back to the seasons of heartbreak that I had, I can remember moments that are very specific. Some were joyful memories and some were painful.

I remember a moment that I was on my knees in prayer, begging God to fix what had been broken. I remember the tears hitting the floor. I remember shortness of breath. I remember the confusion swirling in my head. I remember feeling crushed. And I also remember a song that was playing on my speaker. One of the things that I quickly learned in my grieving is that I needed to constantly listen to worship music. It would remind my head and my heart to sing and mediate on the words of life that Jesus offers.

I remember that as I was praying, begging, grieving, mourning, and lamenting with God, I heard a lyric that made me stop in my tracks. It said this: *"Jesus, make new wine out of me."*

New wine? What could that mean? Something about this prayer from this song lyric blew me away in this moment. "Wait a second", I thought. "Jesus could want to make something *new* out of me?"

My goal in this chapter is to help you learn something that took me a long road of hurt and confusion to learn. Here is it: In heartache, the crushing is inevitable. Unfortunately, you will be crushed, and God will allow you to be.

Why does he allow crushing? Is it because He is a bad God? Is it because He doesn't love you? Is it because He can't identify with pain and hurt? Absolutely not!

In Isaiah 53:5, we see how much our God can identify with this feeling: *"But he was pierced for our rebellion, **crushed** for our sins. He was beaten so we could be whole. He was whipped so we could be healed."*

Why was Jesus crushed? To make something **new** happen:

New purpose

New covenant

New freedom

New hope

New life

Jesus wasn't crushed so that He could try to rebuild or recreate what was there. God allowed for Him to go through a season of crushing so that something new, that had never been there before, could be created.

My hope is that you could begin to believe that God may be allowing a season of crushing to happen in your life, but not so that you could just try to rebuild what has been broken. Instead, you could begin to believe that He is allowing the crushing to create something new in you.

When wine is created, grapes have to be crushed. They have to be fully removed from the shape and the mold that they were "comfortable" being in. After the crushing, the process isn't over. The crushed grapes then have to enter into a process of fermentation for two to three weeks before the new product, wine, is created.

If you are unfamiliar with the word or process of fermentation, it's when the sugars in the grapes are eaten away by yeast, turning it into alcohol. It eats away what is no longer needed in the grape to turn it into its new purpose.

This is why I love the comparison between the season of crushing that we might walk through to that of a grape in the process of becoming wine, because often, the process to God creating something new in us will look similar.

We will be picked from a vine that we think was bringing us life, even though most times it was actually leading us away from the life we were created for. Then, we walk through a really hard season of crushing. It hurts. It hits us in places we didn't think we'd be hit. It brings out things in us we didn't know were there, and by the end of the crushing, it can feel like there's nothing left that we recognize. And then do we instantly become the new that God is creating us? Absolutely not. It takes weeks, months, even years, of eating away at what God no longer needs in us, to begin creating the new that He has purposed for us to begin walking in.

What I am saying here is that in the process of stepping into the new that God's turning you into may take a season of sitting in the crushing so that He can transform you into who He wants you to become. I mean look back as Jesus! He was crushed, but then did He automatically become His resurrected self? No! He had to spend three days in a tomb, dead to the life He once knew.

But three days later, He resurrected! Was He the same? No! He was no longer fully man and fully God. He was fully God, ready to retake the throne of Heaven. So, if we find ourselves in a season of being crushed or a season of fermentation, we should be encouraged and hopeful for what is to come, because we serve a faithful God who constantly gives good gifts to His children. So even in the hurt, we can set our eyes on the future. Why? Because the crushing is **just** a season. The stripping away is **just** a season. Newness is on the horizon.

The song that was playing on my speaker that day in my room is a song by *Hillsong Worship* called *New Wine*. The chorus in the song says this:

Make me a vessel, make me an offering, make me whatever you want me to be. I came here with nothing but all you have given me. Jesus make new wine out of me.

Often times, in seasons of crushing, I have realized that they are most painful and last the longest when I keep resisting the thing that God may be trying to do in and through me in the midst of the crushing. I often don't seek after why crushing is taking place. Instead, I just try to sneak my way out of it.

But instead of asking God to get us out of it, what if we began to open our hands and surrender? What if we began to actually ask God to make us whatever He wants us to be?

I think the prayer that many of us need to begin to pray is this: "God, crush and fully destroy anything that is in me, that is not of you. I open up all of my life, lay aside all of my pride, let go of anything I am holding onto, and ask you to make me new, in you."

What I have learned is that crushing leads to purpose. Refining brings transformation. When you lose someone you love, it isn't a question if you are being transformed are not. God is transforming you right now in some way, into to someone new. So, the question is, what are you being transformed into?

What I can confidently say is that we don't have the choice on if we are going to be transformed or not when we are grieving loss and processing hurt. We can't control that. But what God does allow us to control is the things we allow to be the ingredients in the transformation process.

One option you have is to turn to alcohol or another substance. Or you may turn to sleeping all day, a rebound relationship or an internet fling. Or maybe you turn to the friends that you know will never ask any hard questions and aren't centered in Jesus. Those are options as ingredients. But what kind of transformation would those ingredients lead to? I'd venture to guess that they would transform you into a version of yourself that you wouldn't be able to recognize anymore, a version that could lead to years of hurt and trying to recover from.

Another option that you have to turn to, another list of ingredients available, is praying to God about the things you talk to yourself about (so everything). Also, reading the Living Word of God and allowing those truths to transform your mind (aka the Bible) is crucial to transformation. Daily releasing the things you need to release to a God who is bigger than any doubt we have helps to free you from the weight and pressure of trying to maintain control. Lastly, get around people who know the heart of God so that they can speak that heart over you. What kind of transformation could that lead to? I can speak from experience and say that it will also transform you into a version of yourself that you won't recognize, but in the greatest way imaginable.

Grief stage 7: **The Upward Turn**

Another stage of grief that you may go through is called the upward turn. The upward turn is the beginning of finally getting to a place of acceptance in the process of your grief. It is when you begin to believe that things actually could begin to get back to normal soon enough. Regardless of the ingredients that you choose in the process of your transformation, you will eventually end up at the upward turn, on the way to acceptance. The question is, do you want to crawl into that place, potentially hurt and damaged, or do you want to walk into it in confidence because you have discovered a hope that is bigger than your current circumstances? Jesus wants to show you a hope that your heart and your soul are longing to find. But hope comes through the process of abiding in Him. Abiding throughout the fermentation process of your crushing will lead to a wine that is better than you could imagine. I love the bridge of the song *New Wine*. It says:

'Cause where there is new wine, there is new power. There is new freedom, and the Kingdom is here. I lay down my old flames to carry Your new fire today.

Through abiding in Jesus, He is transforming you into a person of freedom, a new freedom. What the enemy wants to do in moments of heartache is to make you believe that the only freedom you can have is by finding another relationship or by getting the person back. He wants you to think that your freedom is dependent on your circumstances. What Jesus wants to show you, however, is that your freedom is determined not by your circumstances, but by the cross. There is *new* freedom He wants to reveal in you.

But there is also new power through the new fire that He wants to build in your life. One of the ways that Jesus wants to reveal the new power He wants to give to you is by narrowing down the lenses that you look through. What do I mean by that? Well, the power of God is the same yesterday, today, and forever. So, when we "unlock" or "discover" more of God's power, that just simply means that God is narrowing and clarifying the lenses that we look through so that we see less of us and less of the things of the world and more of Him and more of the things of Heaven.

In the process of transformation that God has you in right now, He wants to narrow and clarify the lenses that you see through so that you can see Him more clearly and understand the power that you have access to, through faith in Him and His Holy Spirit.

Galatians 5 talks about the power that we have in the presence of Jesus through what is called the Fruit of the Spirit. Every time you walk through a fire or endure crushing to bring about transformation, if you abide in Jesus, it will lead to a clearer view of the Fruit of the Spirit in your life. This means that you'll see real love more clearly. You'll develop a joy that doesn't fade. You'll understand true peace more deeply. You'll view patience differently. You'll have a sharpened view of God's kindness and goodness. You'll rediscover the Lord's faithfulness and learn how to be more faithful. You'll be prepared to walk into relationships with greater gentleness, and you will learn how to maintain better self-control. Doesn't that sound like everything your heart and your soul are longing to find?

The new wine that Jesus is making out of you is a form of you with new freedom and new power. If you allow Him to, He will show you more and more of Him, showing you that you need less of what the world has to offer. Why? Because He is more than enough.

To begin finding acceptance, you need to begin to believe that you don't need a significant other for your life and your purpose to be complete. Now am I saying you should never get married? No. I think that for most people, God has a beautiful marriage and awesome spouse for you one day and your marriage will glorify God and build His Kingdom. But your purpose and your life can't be centered around seeking after that. It has to be centered around Jesus.

To be honest and vulnerable with you, I believe that God allowed me to be crushed twice through hard break-ups because parts of me were putting the girl and the prospect of marriage above Jesus and how He wanted me to build His Kingdom. So He allowed me to be crushed. Again, is it because He is mean and bad? No! It's because He is a Perfect Father who knew that the love and joy I was searching to find in the prospect of marriage could only be found in Him. So I had to go through crushing and transformation more than once. Now being on the other side of it, I'd go through it again to be the product He has created me into. If you are like me and are pretty stubborn, I hope you can learn what it took a couple seasons of crushing for me to learn: Jesus loves when we approach Him in openness and humility. He wants for us to learn to boast in our weaknesses so that His power can be made strong through us.

Jesus, make new wine out of me. This simple, yet powerful prayer can change so much. If you feel like you have been ripped off of the vine of comfort and thrown into a season of crushing you weren't ready for, it's time to begin praying this. *Jesus, make new wine out of me.* And on the other side, you will be so glad that you did.

IT'S TIME...
AND IT'S OKAY
THAT IT IS

ow that you have began to turn your perspective from pain and into purpose, it's time to begin to talk acceptance. The last stage of grief is actually not grieving anymore. It is looking forward to hope. It is accepting that it's over, it's okay that it's over, and now it's time to focus on hope.

God's plans for you are plans that lead to a future and a hope. It's His promise to us. So let's talk the last stage of grief.

*Grief Stage 8: **Acceptance and Hope***

Let me be clear from the start about acceptance. This doesn't necessarily mean that you are just fully moved on, fully healed and fully over it. It doesn't mean you are just forgetting everything about the person or everything that you have been walking through. It doesn't mean that the stage of life you just came from was just a waste.

Acceptance means that you have gotten to a place, in your processing, where you are ready to begin looking forward to what God has next.

But in order to focus on what God has next for you, it is important to be able to begin seeing through the lens of the future God has prepared for you. What do I mean? I mean shifting your eyes towards hope. Instead of holding bitterness towards the person who you are no longer with, begin taking notes of the positive experiences you had with them. This will help you take the positive into the next relationship God has planned for you.

In most cases, the person you were dating wasn't all bad. There was a reason that you dated them in the first place, right? Maybe they were really good and making you feel valued. Maybe they were good at communication. Maybe they were funny. Maybe they had an infectious smile. Maybe you loved how they treated your friends and family. Of course, there were things about them that you didn't love. There's a reason they are a part of your past, not your future.

But they weren't all bad! I think too often, when we begin to look towards the future coming off of a breakup, we fully associate that past experience with the negative parts of it. We focus on the reason it ended. We focus on some hurtful words that were said. We focus on the bad qualities that the person had. I get it. Focusing on the negative and reminding yourself why it ended can help you reach a place of closure. But focusing on what was good can help build a foundation to what you are looking for in the person God has for you for the future.

For example, if they were great at encouraging you but were not so great and following through on commitments, then allow God to use that to help you see who is in the future for you. They should still be great at encouraging you, but also great at following through on commitments. I encourage you to make a list of qualities that you have learned you love having in someone you are dating. Then, make a list of qualities that you have learned you long to have in someone you are dating. Because could it be that God is helping open your eyes to the qualities you will one day find in the spouse He has for you?

Acceptance doesn't mean forgetting. Acceptance means moving towards a future and a hope.

The summer after my sophomore year of high school, I went to Eswatini, South Africa for a mission trip. While we were there, we stayed about 45 minutes away from where we were doing mission. So everyday, we would load onto a bus and head off down dirt roads and winding roads until we got to the homestead where we were sharing the gospel for the day.

I remember there was this one morning where we were headed to a church that we were serving for the day and we left really early to head up there. So naturally, I fell asleep on the bus. When I woke up, we were, all of a sudden, on a mountain, driving along the edge of a cliff. But as we looked out into the valley, all we could see was fog. It looked like we were driving through a cloud.

See, I knew what I was looking out at was beautiful, but all I could see was fog. I knew that where we were going was going to be awesome but all my eyes saw was fog.

You may be thinking:*"Okay Sean, I am ready to walk towards a hope. But what is this hope? What am I hoping in?"* It can be hard to focus on the future and on hope because they can seem so foggy. The past? It's clear. I know what that looked like. I know how that felt. I know what that led to. The present? Yep. I know where I am at right now. I know what is in front of my eyes and what thoughts are in my head. I know the way life looks. I can see it tangibly.

But the future? Not as clear. It's tough because we aren't fortune tellers. We aren't psychics. We don't have some portal into the future that brings us peace and comfort knowing what's coming. Heck, we don't know what's coming tomorrow? So how in the world do we have hope looking towards something that we can't see?

Two of the verses in Scripture that helped me shift my perspective on this was a verse in Romans 8. Romans 8:24-25 says *"Now hope that is seen is not hope. For who hopes for what he sees? But if we hope for what we do not see, we wait for it with patience."*

We don't hope in something that we can see. We hope in the unseen. After your favorite team wins the championship and you are celebrating, you don't scream out: "I hope they win the championship!" You don't hope for a Christmas present after you have already been gifted it. In the same way, after you marry your future spouse, you won't constantly pray and say to God: "I hope I find my spouse soon!" If you do, you need marriage counseling!

We don't hope in what is already seen. We hope in what we believe is coming. So what is coming? Well, only the Lord has the full answer to that question. But what I do know is that of you trust in Him in the journey from here until you get there, what's coming is a spouse that will be supportive. What's coming is a spouse that will love you for who you are and grow and stretch you to look more like Jesus. What's coming could be a marriage centered on Scripture and built on the cornerstone of Christ. What's coming is redemption for what has been lost and healing for what has been broken. What's coming is renewed purpose for you, expanded ministry that you can walk into, and a con-tinually developing testimony of power that God's given you to build His Kingdom.

We can hope in what is coming because we are living under the power and authority of a God who is faithful and who promises good things for His kids.

In my experience, hoping can become the easier part of the equa-tion. The next part is difficult: waiting for it with patience.

Let's be honest…many times, when we get to a place of acceptance, we are ready to move on. Moving on is good. But too often, when we think of moving on, we think of moving on in to another relationship. But what if God wants to do a beautiful work within your season of singleness? The Lord majorly convicted me on this one. I won't go into a full rant on singleness, because there are great resources out there for that already. My favorite is a book called *Single, Dating, Engaged, Married* by Ben Stuart. I highly recommend it.

The one thing that I will say on waiting patiently is this: as followers of Jesus, we should be dating for marriage, right? So let me ask you a question that I feel the Lord convicted me on. *Have you gotten what God need you to get out of your singleness?* Notice I said God, not you. I was living in a space where I kept evaluating if I felt like I got what I needed out of singleness, but I had it so backwards. Instead, Jesus taught me that I need to begin to ask Him: Lord, have I gotten out what you have planned for me to learn in my singleness?

This question is so crucial because if you think about it, this could be the last season that you are single in your life. If you are dating for marriage, then the person you date next could be your future spouse. So if that's true, this is the last chance for you to learn what Jesus needs you to learn as you walk into your future marriage. So do not rush it. It may seem like a long road, but in the grand scheme of things, this season will just be a blink of an eye. Wait with patience. I promise you that it will be worth every moment of the waiting.

At this point we have walked through each stage of grief. Again, you may not experience all of these stages as you journey towards healing. Everyone processes grief differently. If you haven't yet reached acceptance and hope, this is the time where you continually pray for the Lord to help your heart get to a place of looking towards the future and towards hope.

I want to give you a space to pause and pray before we move into these final two chapters. If you have reached acceptance, are beginning your journey of singleness, and are looking towards the future with hope, then use this space to praise Jesus for getting you here and begin to ask the Lord to reveal what He wants to teach you in your singleness. If you are still wresting and battling, pray the Lord would bring you closure and heal what is still broken or bitter.

Regardless of where you are, your Heavenly Father longs to hear your real, genuine words. Take some time and talk to Him.

_____

_____

_____

_____

_____

_____

_____

_____

_____

_____

_____

_____

_____

_____

_____

_____

_____

_____

_____

_____

_____

_____

LETTER OF ENCOURAGEMENT

'm a words of affirmation guy. Are you? I will be honest. I don't know if I have ever met someone who has ever said "You know what, I feel way too encouraged today" or "I'd really like for you to stop saying nice things to me…could you be a little meaner?" I don't think very often we just long for someone to discourage us.

In seasons of heartbreak and hurt and processing, so often my heart and my soul just needed to be encouraged. So I wanted to make sure to take a little time to encourage you. I know I may not know you personally, but I do know some truths about you because they are truths that the God of the Universe thinks about you.

I want to take some time to speak these truths over you and write them so that you will read them and reread them and reread until they become truth for you to.

You ready? Here we go.

My friend…

You are loved.

You are loved by the God of the Universe. You are loved by the One whose name is Love. You are loved so much that someone has died for you so that pain doesn't have to be the end of your story. And God has a love for you that you haven't uncovered yet. It may be a love through the future marriage that He has for you with an earthly spouse. But it will definitely be a perfect love that you will experience every moment of every day in eternity with your perfect, loving Father.

You are worthy.

You are worthy of pursuit. You are worthy of not having to change the personality that God has gifted you with to make another person happier. You are worthy of being affirmed. You are worthy of love. You are worthy of joy. You are worthy of pursuit. You are worthy of being seen. You have been made worthy of the cross through Jesus, who humbly gave Himself over to death so that you could be made worthy of life. You are worthy.

You are enough.

You are not defined by the mistakes that you made in your last relationship. You are not defined by the sin that you have fallen into. You are not looked at as your past. Through Jesus, you are enough. The spouse that God has for you one day will look at you, who you are in Jesus, as enough too. Does that mean that you won't change in your eventual marriage? Absolutely not. But it means that you will change to look even more like Jesus, not forced to change in a way that is opposite of the character and gifts that God has intentionally crafted in you.

You are seen.

I know in times like these, it can feel like you are very unseen. It can be easy to feel that way because you aren't getting texts or calls or getting to see the person you were dating anymore, so you feel unseen.

As loneliness creeps in, your thoughts begin to make you believe that no one sees you or the pain that you are walking through. But this isn't true. You are seen. Scripture shows over and over that you are always seen.

Jeremiah 12:3: *But you, O Lord, know me; you see me, and test my heart toward you.*

Psalm 33:18: *But the eyes of the LORD are on those who fear him, on those whose hope is in his unfailing love.*

2 Chronicles 16:9: *The eyes of the LORD search the whole earth in order to strengthen those whose hearts are fully committed to him.*

Isaiah 41:10: *So do not fear, for I am with you; do not be dismayed, for I am your God. I will strengthen you and help you; I will uphold you with my righteous right hand.*

Psalm 121:8: *The LORD will watch over your coming and going both now and forevermore.*

God knows the number of every hair that is on your head. He intimately knows and sees you.

You are seen.

You are heard.

My friend, your prayers are not coming up empty. You are not just speaking to the air. You will see the fruition of every thing that you are praying for. It may not look exactly like what you are asking for. But however He answers, it will look better that anything you could have ever asked for, dreamt of, or imagined because that is the kind of God you are speaking to. God hears your every thought before you even think them, the good and the bad, And He loves you in the midst of every one of them. You are heard.

You are not alone.

You may feel like you are alone right now. Like losing that person left you lost and without your best friend. You may have ran in the same circles and had the same friend groups and now that your relationship is over, you feel alone, even by who you thought would be your support system. Again, you are not alone. The Holy Spirit dwells within you and leads and guides you every single step of the way towards healing and redemption. As far as friends go, if they aren't there for you in the midst of your hurt, regardless of who is involved in it, then that speaks more of their character than yours. You are not alone and there are people God has for your life that will make sure you know and believe that you are not alone. If you aren't plugged into your local church, I believe God can use this as a hub to find the people that will fight for you and with you. You are not alone.

This is not the end. It's just the beginning.

Sometimes we have to walk through necessary endings in order to step into the new beginnings God has for us. Yes, something has ended. But something else has just begun, and the beginning of what is to come is so much better than what has just ended.

These phrases are great. But at first read, your heart and mind may not believe them for you yet. Because of this, I am going to write these in first person, so that when you read them, you say it about yourself. You have to claim it for you.

So claim it, in Jesus' name.

I am loved.

God's love for me is patient and kind. God's love for me is not jealous or boastful or proud or rude. It does not demand its own way. God's love for me is not irritable, and it keeps no record of being wronged. God does not rejoice about injustice but rejoices whenever the truth wins out. God's love never gives up on me, never loses faith in me, is always hopeful, and endures through every circumstance. (1 Corinthians 13:4-7)

I am worthy.

I have been crucified with Christ. It is no longer I who live, but Christ who lives in me. And the life I now live in the flesh I live by faith in the Son of God, who loved me and gave himself for me. (Galatians 2:20)

I am enough.

But he said to me, "My grace is sufficient for you, for my power is made perfect in weakness." Therefore I will boast all the more gladly about my weaknesses, so that Christ's power may rest on me. That is why, for Christ's sake, I delight in weaknesses, in insults, in hardships, in persecutions, in difficulties. For when I am weak, then I am strong. (2 Corinthians 12:9-10)

I am seen.

I will not fear, for Jesus is with me. I will not be dismayed, for Jesus is my God. He will strengthen me and help me; he will uphold me with His righteous right hand. (Isaiah 41:10)

I am heard.

I know that God promises that if I call to Him, He will answer me, and will tell me great and hidden things that I have not known. (Jeremiah 33:3)

So I will call upon Him and come and pray to Him, and He will hear me. I will seek Him and find Him, when I seek Him with all my heart. (Jeremiah 29:12-13)

I am not alone.

I can be strong and courageous! I do not have to be afraid and do not have panic. For the LORD my God will personally go ahead of me He will neither fail me nor abandon me. (Deuteronomy 31:6)

This is just the beginning for me.

For God knows the plans He has for me. They are plans to prosper me and not to harm me. The plans that God has for me are plans to give me hope and a future better than anything I can imagine. (Jeremiah 29:11)

Sometimes we just need a place to constantly come back to to remind ourselves of what God believes for each of us. I hope this can be a letter of encouragement to your heart and your mind, so that you can counteract the schemes of the enemy and write truth over any lies you've been believing.

Be encouraged. You are being fought for because you are worthy of being fought for.

THE REDEMPTION PLAN

So…where do I go from here?

remember asking that question over and over again. I had got through the pain of processing, the process of crushing, the stages of grief, and I finally got to acceptance. Not only acceptance, but hope. Yet still, I didn't fully know where to go from the place of acceptance and begin to walk in the place of hope.

So I figured that we could develop a redemption plan together. How does that sound? In order to do this, there is a story that I need you to be familiar with from the Bible because it is, quite literally, the foundation that we will build this plan on.

The story comes from Jesus's teaching in Matthew 7. He tells the story in the form of a parable, which is a story that has a deeper meaning within it to be uncovered.

This is what He says:

"Everyone then who hears these words of mine and does them will be like a wise man who built his house on the rock. And the rain fell, and the floods came, and the winds blew and beat on that house, but it did not fall, because it had been founded on the rock. And everyone who hears these words of mine and does not do them will be like a foolish man who built his house on the sand. And the rain fell, and the floods came, and the winds blew and beat against that house, and it fell, and great was the fall of it."

The first part of walking in the redemption plan that God has for you is by never moving from building on the foundation of rock. Jesus teaches here that we have two options of foundations to stand on and begin to build our life on: rock or sand. To be honest, there were moments after a break-up where I thought I was standing fully on the rock of Jesus as my foundation. But when I went through the loss, and the house I had built came crashing down, I quickly realized one foot may be on rock, but the other was clearly still standing on sand.

When I was in high school, my student pastor said something once that ten years later, I still go back to. He said this line:

"When your foundation is stable, your world doesn't have to be."

This means that when your life is fully built on the person of Jesus, you have a foundation that will never fall, regardless of the circumstances that you walk through. It's in moments of collapse, however, that I have realized many times that my foundation has not been as stable as I thought it was.

Before you begin to rebuild, you need to check the foundation that you are building on. The foundation is the most important part.

A famous hymn sings:

On Christ the solid rock I stand
All other ground is sinking sand
All other ground is sinking sand

When we try to build on any foundation, other than the foundation of rock, that is Jesus, we are building on sinking sand. We are building on a foundation that is destined to make our lives crumble at some point, because the foundation is unstable.

When I was a kid, I remember my mom and my dad telling me the story of the three little pigs and the big bad wolf. Do you remember this story? My parents loved this story so much that one year for Halloween, my mom dressed me up as the big bad wolf and my dad and his two friends up as the three "little" pigs. This is a moment where you pray and praise Jesus that this isn't in a picture book because I looked straight up terrifying.

If you grew up under a rock, let me give you a quick recap of the story. Basically there are three pigs and they are building a house to live in. Life is pretty great for a while there, as they are chilling in their house, comfortable. But then a threat comes to destroy the life that they knew so well: the big bad wolf.

And for the first time, the supplies that the pigs used to build their houses mattered because the structures of their houses were in jeopardy. One of the pigs built their house out of straw and so when the big bad wolf came and blew with all of his might, the houses collapsed, and the pig was left out, vulnerable to the enemy. The second pig built his of sticks, and the same result happened: collapse and vulnerability to danger.

But the third pig had a different story. Why? Because he built his house out of brick. So when the big bad wolf blew and blew and blew, nothing happened to the house. The third pig was protected from the enemy.

The materials that they built with changed everything. And in the same way, the materials that we rebuild our house with matters. We may not feel how much it matters at first. There may be a season of comfort. But one day, the enemy will come to try to destroy what we have been building again. This is why you need to learn to build your house proactively, so that there never comes a moment where you aren't ready to react to whatever attack comes against you.

Once we know we have the firm foundation, the materials we build with are the next step. So what materials do we need to use to build into the redemption plan that God has for us? I want to walk through a couple, the two that the pig that survived must have used to build.

1) The Bricks

The bricks that we need to use to build are the spiritual disciplines that lead us daily back to Jesus. What are the essential elements of spiritual disciplines?.

One brick to stack is prayer. Prayer is talking to Jesus about what you are talking to yourself about. So talk to Him about what you're stressed about, what you're pumped about, how you're feeling, what you're thinking. He longs to hear from you. Journal your prayers, say your prayers out loud, turn your car into a prayer room and really talk and process with the Lord.

Another brick to stack is Scripture. The Bible is a way Jesus longs to speak to you. This is the way that we learn more about the character of our God. Get in a Bible plan with someone on the Bible app. It is a great resource. Commit to find a time and a place to read every day and watch as God uses these bricks to give you words of life to build the next chapter of your life on.

Another brick to stack is to invite the Spirit into your day. Jesus gave us a gift in the Holy Spirit to be our helper and direct our path. Every day, look through your schedule for that day and invite the Holy Spirit to move how He needs to. This can look like saying: "Holy Spirit today I have this meeting or this conversation with this person. Would you give me boldness and clarity on the words to say?" Or it could look like, "Holy Spirit today I have this test or this meeting or this phone call, would you give me the fruits of the Spirit of patience and love and teach me the steps to take." The Holy Spirit can often be a neglected part of the way we build, but He is essential to the building process. Invite Him in.

Another brick to stack, as you build, is silent solitude. Man, if I can be honest, this one is the hardest for me. But in the seasons that I actually am obedient enough to practice it, it can be one of the most powerful. Often times, we can be good at talking but we get upset when we feel like Jesus isn't speaking to us. What I have learned is that many times, when I feel like God has been silent, I am not carving out time to sit in silence with Him and just listen. Let this be a brick you build with.

The last brick is worship. Listen to worship in your car, your room, and your AirPods at school or work. Let these lyrics of power speak over you and remind your mind of Jesus. Even at the gym, I hear you get the biggest lifts in of your life if you listen to worship on repeat. In your hurt, the enemy wants to speak lies. But worship music helps to shower your mind with truth and help your mind to believe what is being said.

Spiritual disciplines are so crucial to the redemption plan that God has for you. Want to know why? Because when you spend daily time with Him and build with these bricks, you give Him room to speak to you, to direct your paths, to remind you who you are in Him, and to keep your eyes on the coming future and the coming hope that He has for you. But when bricks are built in a house, they need something to hold them together and seal them into place. This is when the mortar comes into play.

2) The Mortar

What does your support system look like right now? How are the encouraging you? How are the challenging you? How are they helping you evaluate your foundation? How are they helping you look toward the future? How are they reminding you of your hope?

I cannot over emphasize how crucial the community that you lean into and allow to have a platform to speak into your life, especially during heart break, is. One of my favorite pastors and authors, Craig Groeschel, once wrote this challenging statement: *"Show me your friends, and I'll show you your future. The people you're hanging out with today are shaping the person you will become tomorrow."*

As you move forward to where God is leading you to go next, you need to make sure you are moving forward alongside the people who will help lead you to the future you want. The friends closest to you will play an integral part in shaping you will become tomorrow and for years to come.

If I can be honest with you, outside of the grace of Jesus, the only reason I was able to heal well and move forward from my heartbreak was because of the friends that I had in my life. I have three really close guy friends who pushed me to love Jesus more by holding me accountable to keep my eyes on Him. They gave me hard truth when I needed it, a hug when I needed one, and constantly prayed with me and for me. They would read Scripture over me. They'd remind me of my purpose and the gifts God had given me. They were always down for a hang when I got lonely. No matter what my day looked like, my emotions felt like or what my thoughts said, I knew they'd be constant because they had their eyes so fully on Jesus. Can you say these things confidently about the friends that are closest to you? If not, your bricks could become wobbly.

Listen, I have friends who don't follow Jesus too. They are great. They are fun. They help take my mind off of heartbreak too. They are great encouragers too. But the foundation that they stand on is different than the one that I stand on and is different than the foundation I want to be standing on for the rest of my life. Friends who don't have a relationship with Jesus won't help you build a house of bricks, built on an immovable foundation. Their house will look more like a straw house built on sand.

And it's not because they don't have good intentions! They just don't have the same hope that followers of Jesus do. They haven't been introduced to Jesus or haven't surrendered to Him yet. So they just don't have the same materials to build with. You need to have friends in your corner who are building with the same supplies and can teach you how to build too.

The future that God has for you is one that is built on the foundation of Jesus. The house that God has prepared for you to live in for years to come is full of spiritual disciplines that will shape your character and drive your hope. And it is full of friends that will challenge you, encourage you, help you look more like Jesus and point you to the redemption plan that is coming.

Friend, I know this season has been a difficult one and it can feel like the story that is never ending. But I want to leave you with this reminder: This is just a short chapter in the story that Jesus is writing in your life.

A friend of mine once told me something years ago that I have held onto since and I want to share it with you. I hope that this statement will bring you hope to know that this is just the beginning of the redemption plan that Jesus has for you:

You will know the redemption plan God has for you the moment you see your wife walking down the aisle to you. All of the pain will be worth it in that moment.

Friend, there will come a day when all of this pain will be worth it. The day you see your husband at the end of the aisle or you see your wife walking down the aisle to you will be a moment where you'll know its been worth it. And until that day and through that day, let this truth be the anthem that we command our hearts and minds to know:

"For I know the plans I have for you,' declares the Lord,
'plans to prosper you and not to harm you, plans to give
you a hope and a future." (Jeremiah 29:11)

You are in the hands of the Creator of the Universe. He is bigger
than your doubts, your pain and your processing, and He promises a
future full of hope for you. That is something that we can believe and
hold onto!

If you love someone...you have to be able to set them free. But in
the midst of it, if you believe Jesus is who He says He is...you have to
be able to believe that freedom is available to you too.

About the Author

Sean Curry is a pastor in Alpharetta, Georgia. He is an avid
Swiftie and New York sports fan. He has a passion to help
lead the next generation of students and leaders to be bold
and courageous in and for the name of Jesus. He currently
serves as the Student Pastor for Stonecreek Church.

Made in the USA
Middletown, DE
05 June 2023

31891745R00083